# OPTING
## FOR OPULENCE

### 14 Proven Strategies to Master Selling in the Luxury Market

## Greg Winston

NEW YORK

Opting For Opulence
© 2009 Greg Winston. All rights reserved.

| | | |
|---|---|---|
| Hardcover | ($29.97) | 1-60037-509-X / 9781600375095 |
| Paperback | ($16.95) | 1-60037-510-3 / 9781600375101 |
| eBook | ($19.97) | 1-60037-511-1 / 9781600375118 |

**Published by:**

MORGAN · JAMES™

THE ENTREPRENEURIAL PUBLISHER

www.morganjamespublishing.com

Morgan James Publishing, LLC
1225 Franklin Ave. Ste 325
Garden City, NY 11530-1693
Toll Free 800-485-4943
www.MorganJamesPublishing.com

**Cover & Interior Design by:**
Tennyson Rog
www.rogdesigns.com
tennyson@rogdesigns.com

In an effort to support local communities, raise awareness and funds, Morgan James Publishing donates one percent of all book sales for the life of each book to Habitat for Humanity.
Get involved today, visit
**www.HelpHabitatForHumanity.org.**

# Dedication

To the sales warriors!

The people who represent sales organizations all over the world. The people who have taken the act of selling to a level of true professionalism.

To those intelligent selling executives who look at the art of selling as a continuous educational process, as they:

Prepare each week for a week better than the last week.

- **Go through countless "no's" as they strive for their personal goals**

- **Brave the weather in its sometimes good, most time unpredictable almost always changing impact**

- **And for those who endure the "selling" stigma as they demonstrate to the world that … everyone sells something – we just prefer to sell at the highest level of professionalism.**

# Testimonial

Dear Greg,

Not sure where to begin, so I should probably start with "Thank you."

What an incredible couple of days – lent in great part to your participation.

I had a sense from the time we met first on the phone that I was in the presence of someone special – and my intuition served me well.

You not only exude a warmth personally, but you find a way to marry it with a keen sense of business acuity that makes you truly unique.

Your concepts and insight were wonderfully conveyed with an heir of confidence and humor that I rarely experience. You were spot-on – and the audience was rapt.

My only reservation on your presentation was

that it wasn't more widely seen. We will be able to rectify that on Friday.

I look forward to a long and mutually beneficial relationship and would be honored to present you and your services to other members, chapters and colleagues around the world.

I end the way I began, with a heartfelt thank you.

Kind regards,

*David M. Winter*

David M. Winters
President
The Luxury Marketing Council Southern California (LuxeSC)

# Acknowledgements

**Gia Winston,** thank you for your obvious love. Life would be so difficult without the joy you bring me.

**Lewis Weiss,** my friend whose sales life was instrumental in starting my sales life. Our friendship has covered 30 years and will go on forever.

**Keith Harrell,** motivation, friendship, inspiration and more. You are not a secret anymore and I only hope the rest of the world gets a chance see and feel what major companies all over the world have experienced.

**Rebecca Lafferty,** to have it all must be exhausting. I love and appreciate you for everything you do to keep me going.

**Tennyson Rog,** an artist who's time has finally come. This concept is only possible because of you.

**Randy Gilbert,** for your time, energy and guidance.

**Greg Whitsett,** the "Pond Guy" who went from client to friend. You are among the few who inspire me.

**"Dot" Missett,** for your inspiration and support - Go Michigan!

# A Brief Excerpt from

## Opting for Opulence

Fear seems to be a natural reaction in salespeople. It was in me. Somehow, I felt afraid when I began my sales career. There was always a mixture of emotions. I felt like I was imposing. I felt like I was somehow tricking potential customers. It didn't matter the product. I felt that people were doing me a favor if they bought it.

As a child I sold newspapers on a street corner. I remember a hot summer evening standing near a traffic light. As shiny late-model cars filled with executives and families passed me going home, I would hold up the latest edition and shout, "Democrat, get your evening Democrat here." When the cars stopped for the traffic light, I walked down the line of cars holding up a copy of the paper, too nervous to say anything. I would just show the paper.

When the light changed, my confidence came back and I would bellow as loud as I could, "Democrat, get your evening Democrat here." Selling newspapers was my first exposure to sales. For the life of me, I couldn't understand why rich people needed a newspaper or why they needed me to sell it to them.

So there I was, standing on my favorite newspaper corner, right across from the doughnut shop. I could smell the fresh doughnut dough. Soon, I knew that I could finish selling papers and run across the street for my favorite doughnut, chocolate-filled glazed. Oh, I could just feel the chocolate oozing out as I took my first bite. One or two more bites, and I'd wash it down with milk so cold it would cause brain-freeze.

As I snapped back to reality I saw that the light had turned red, and one of the rich people was talking to me as he rolled down the window of his air-conditioned car. I looked at him with that non-blinking, reptilian-like stare and he shouted again over the noise of traffic, "HEY KID … DO YOU HAVE AN EXTRA?" "No," I said." He looked at me in disbelief.

The light changed, and he drove off.

I stood there motionless. Oh my God, I thought, he wanted a paper. I was so nervous around people and selling that my brain shut down. I had a stack of newspapers. I certainly knew what the word extra meant, but fear caused my doughnut-focused mind to shut down.

While it may have appeared that I functioned on the outside, my inside mechanisms had stalled. Fear is the greatest enemy of selling professionals. It holds us back, it slows us down and it causes us to miss life's greatest opportunities.

Before there can be consistent, reliable growth in the selling process, you first have to have consistent, reliable growth as a person. Fear stifles our talent. It causes us not to do what we know we can.

Fear blocks our progress…

# Table of Contents

**Prologue**
**Opportunity Knocks Twice**                                           1

**Introduction**
**Selling to The Select Few**                                          7
   The Only Question Worth Asking                        8
   What IS The New Luxury Mindset?                      10
   Selling Today                                        12
   Let's Get Physical:
      Body Language, Then & Now           14
   Memo From The Future:
      Selling to the New Luxury Mindset    17
   The Wrong Approach for the Right Audience:
      Targeting the New Luxury Mindset     18

**The 1st Essential**
**Understanding the GIRI Concept of Elite Prospecting**               23
   Create a Proactive Approach                          26
   The "Tie-In"                                         28

**The 2nd Essential**
**Proper Thought**                                                    31
   Build Your Confidence                                34
   Success Is in Our Minds                              37
   Getting More...                                      37

Commission Beats Salary                                40
Insights into Success:
    5 Strategies for Selling to the New Luxury Mindset   42

**The 3rd Essential**
**Personal Magnetism**                                 **47**
    The First Product                                47
    Love Jon Richardson                              47
    What Causes Magnetism?                           49
    People Bonding With People                       50
    Speaker Magnets                                  51
    The Second Movement                              53
    First, Get the Job                               55
    Presentation                                     58

**The 4th Essential**
**Positive Internal Dialogue**                         **65**
    Overcoming Fear                                  66
    The First Movement:
        Self Development                             68
    H.A.B.E.: The 90% Factor                         69
    "If You Want to Be Successful,
        *Don't Watch 60 Minutes!*"                  70
    Rejection                                        73
    Your Journal:
        The Best Book You Ever Read                 74
    Tell Yourself Good Things                        76
    Success Talk                                     76

**The 5th Essential**
**The Time to Sell**                                   **79**
    Don't "Find" Time You Don't Have,
        Manage the Time You Do                       81
    The Top Ten Ways to Get Things Done              83
    Other Sales Observations                         84

**The 6th Essential**
**The Art of Asking Questions**                                     91
   Gathering the Right Information                    91
   The Funnel System                                 93
   The Concept of Dissonance –
      Our Greatest Sales Tool          95
   Tactics for Improved Listening                     97
   The Fear of Loss                                   98

**The 7th Essential**
**Customer Attraction**                                            101
   Customer Growth                                    102
   Phase I: Spring Board Your Relationships           102
   Phase II: Sell, Serve, Repeat!                     103

**The 8th Essential**
**Emotional Advantage**                                            107

**The 9th Essential**
**Perspective**                                                    113
   Perspective                                       113
   The Plan                                           116
   Principles for Better Sales                        123
   Internal Motivation                                132
   Your Master Plan:
      Creating a Blueprint for Success 133
   Four Secrets of Internal Motivation                135
   The Question of Why                                138

**The 10th Essential**
**Scrap History, Sell Illogically!**                               143

**The 11th Essential**
**Brand Logically**                                                149

**The 12th Essential**
**Beliefs are the Bottom Line**                                    155

**The 13th Essential**
**Success Blueprint**                                    **159**
   How To Read The Writing On The Wall,
     Before Its On The Wall                              161
   Career Analysis and Planning                          161
   GIRI Systems:                                         162
   The Most Important Question:
     Am I Willing to do What it Takes
     to Develop the Career I Am Striving For?            163

**The 14th Essential**
**Perpetual Training**                                   **167**
   Lessons from the Street                               168
   A Green Light for Learning                            169
   The New Information                                   170
   Who's Afraid?                                         171

**Prologue**
Opportunity Knocks Twice

# Prologue

## Opportunity Knocks Twice

WHAT a great day! It's just beautiful. All around me are clear skies, the perfect temperature and the sun shining on my face. Sitting down on a park bench, I turn to my right to see a mother and daughter running and playing in the sun.

From the park bench I smile and start to turn away... but the "bang" sound brings me back to the mother and girl.

Gunfire! An unmistakable sound I hadn't heard since we moved out of the housing project... the sound of gang war days. The Mother and child, they are not laughing and playing – there's a man chasing them!

Bang! Bang! The mother falls to the ground, two feet in front of me.

The child stops a few feet to my left, she stares – then she screams. The man is now standing right in front of me. I can't move. All I can think is, "I'm going to die in the park. I'm going to die on a sunny day, in a park... I will die for no reason."

He stands above me. He stares at me for what seems like an hour. The gun is at my eye level. I just look at him.

I'm too afraid to blink; he stares back, and his eyes narrow. Everything, every movement now is in slow motion; the sound of the park is gone; all I hear is my heart beating.

Thump, Thump, Thump – bass drum, punch in the chest – all I hear is my heart. Deafness to everything else, for the first time in my life I can actually hear… fear.

He raises the gun and Bang!

He shoots himself in the head. The force of the bullet pushes his head to one side. There is almost no sign that he has been hit by the bullet and splash, the opposite side of his head bursts open with blood! He falls slowly to the ground.

To my right another man jumps the park fence, rips his jacket off and covers the woman. He glances my way and shouts, "Stay here." He takes his shirt off and covers the head of the man I'm sure is dead; then he rushes to comfort the little girl.

Something tells me to stand up. I taste my tears and realize I am crying. I move to my left and start to walk. My shirt, wet from sweat, is cool on my chest and back. Something tells me that, more than my tears, everything on me is wet.

A mile later, I'm in my front yard and don't remember the walk. I didn't hear sirens, but all of a sudden police surround me.

Mom runs out of the house yelling at the police officers, "Leave him alone!"

The patrolman tries to explain that I am the only witness. "Ma'am we just want to…"

Bam, Bam, Bam! There's a knock at the door! I wake up, relieved that it was all just a dream. It's the same dream; more memory than nightmare. Over 20 years later and it still seems real. At the door is a room service delivery, and I realize I'm at the St. Regis Hotel. I'm in the light of Orange County, California – not in the darkness of the ghetto.

"Come in," I tell the room service attendant, an eager guy whose nametag says "Earl." I tell him, "Please, set up in the living room. How did you know what I wanted?"

"Your assistant ordered for you," Earl explains.

"Oh, long night I guess."

"You're some sort of motivational speaker, I hear?"

"No – not exactly. I help companies understand how to sell luxury items at a higher level of success."

"Wow, do you mind if I ask you a question?"

"You just did."

Earl blushes. "Oh, may I ask another one then?"

"Okay, shoot."

"How did you get to… to do this, to stay in the Presidential suite? I mean, you just look really successful."

"I have been asked that same question many times. Maybe, Earl, maybe I should write the answer in a book…"

---

Here is that book. Here is the story of a boy who became a man; of a man who became a salesman; of a salesman who became an expert in selling to the luxury market. And why not?

I figured if I could come from my background – the highlights of which you've just read – and be a success, why not be a success in the most challenging, demanding and rewarding of markets –

Set goals for what they will make of YOU!

the new luxury mindset?

What is the new luxury mindset? Who is Greg Winston? All in good time, my friends; all in good time. For now know this: this is my story, these are my words.

If I can overcome the grim realities of the ghetto, fight poverty through action and perseverance, and triumph to become a top seller for such companies as Xerox and Warner Brothers, then you can surely attain all the goals you have for yourself in this most rewarding of fields.

Read on for the adventure of a lifetime...

## Introduction
Selling to The Select Few

# Introduction

## Selling to The Select Few

"In bad times, the rich usually get richer."

**Stuart Wilde, author of The Trick to
Money is Having Some!**

The rich keep getting richer.

According to Robert B. Reich, professor of Public Policy
at the University of California at Berkeley and author of
*The Future of Success*, "In recent years, the top fifth of American workers has held 85 percent of the country's wealth…
In China, the wealthiest 5 percent now control half of all
bank deposits."

Household wealth is hitting record heights, and not just
in the U.S. There are more millionaire households on the
planet than ever before, particularly in Europe and in China, where growth rates are highest.

The total number of world millionaire households—
those with assets of $1 million or more—grew by 14% in

2006, 9.6 million, representing the richest 0.7% of all households and owning $33.2 trillion, or about a third of the world's wealth, according to a recent study by the Boston Consulting Group, a global management consulting firm.

Meanwhile the U.S. had, by far, the highest number of million-aire households, with nearly 4.6 million, and the highest number of $100 million-plus households, with 2,300. The number of mil-lionaire households increased by a steady 10%.

So what does this all mean for you, the modern salesman fac-ing bleak times as words like "recession," "cutbacks," "layoffs" and "budget" rear their ugly heads? Simple: the rich are getting richer, so why aren't you joining them?

## The Only Question Worth Asking

Before you read any further ask yourself: Do you *need* to sell or do you *want* to sell? Think carefully about your answer, because it might mean the difference between succeeding or floundering in your approach to reaching what I call "the new luxury mindset." These are people who know what they want; who go out and get it, regardless of cost – without fear, trepidation or indecision.

To sell to the rich, you must think like the rich. So ask yourself:

Do you *need* it?

Or do you *want* it?

A needy salesperson is easy to spot. They've taken a sales job be-cause they have no other options available or because they think it will be an "easy" way to make a living. With visions of leisurely client lunches at fancy restaurants, long weekends spent training at resorts and enormous commission checks, they set out to find their own personal sales style. They tell themselves that they will eventually figure out what works for them. In the meantime they make all kinds of plans to contact prospects, to learn more about their products, even to read more sales books.

Do you *need* to sell or do you *want* to sell?

On the other hand, a salesperson that *wants* it isn't so busy making plans. They know that there's too much to do – right now. They realize that there is neither a right nor a wrong system. Instead, they seek out those who are already selling and imitate their actions and attitudes.

Next they test those behaviors to determine what works best for them. They condense many activities down to "The Essential Strategies" they must embrace for success.

## What IS The New Luxury Mindset?

The new luxury mindset is just that; a mindset rather than a strict geographic, monetary or even statistical interpretation. Many who make up the new luxury mindset are middle class versus upper class.

Explains Carter Turrell of *Forbes* magazine, "While luxury items were once only for the very rich, now even middle-class American consumers are demanding luxury items in a variety of categories, including the obvious ones, such as apparel, accessories, and jewelry, as well as the not-so-obvious, such as food, beverages, and underwear."

You might say it all started with Starbucks and that revolutionary new cup of "designer coffee". Nobody seemed to mind paying four or five bucks when the Seattle company opened its first coffee shop back in 1984, when the company first adopted its progressive "coffee bar culture" concept.

From there, the world of "designer" this and "luxury" that became a sales free-for-all, making way for gourmet fast food, lettuce in bags, personal trainers, titanium luggage, concierge service and luxury car leases.

Just how much is luxury worth? Research from Boston Consulting Group (BCG) indicates that "… consumers today are willing to pay up to ten times conventional price levels for new luxury items."

As one might imagine, this revolutionary new way of thinking is opening tons of opportunities for the forward thinking, aggressive and passionate salesperson. That is why I asked if you needed to sell – or if you wanted to sell.

Clearly, the line between need and want is blurred as you begin to approach the new luxury mindset. Do they *need* a five dollar cup of coffee, four dollar muffin, three dollar tin of designer breath mints, two dollar bendable pencil or one dollar gumball?

Do they *need* to get their clothes dry-cleaned while they play video games or update their Facebook listing on-site, lease a Mercedes Benz, charter a flight to Belize or invest five grand in the latest high-tech gadget for their "man cave"? Doubtful, but clearly they want to – and will want to for the foreseeable future. Your mission, should you choose to accept it, is to make the new luxury mindset your new target market – ASAP.

This book, *Opting for Opulence*, will show you how.

I will use the ongoing sales polls and questionnaires conducted on *www.sales2sales.com*. With an average of 2,000 sales people per research project, this sales site investigates what is working in sales right now.

Observations of the selling arena over the past few years led me to a startling realization that changes in the market happen so rapidly that traditional methods of training tend to fall behind. To sell effectively we must have on-going information that mirrors our clients' buying habits and motivators. In addition, much of that information has to be specific to our industries.

## Selling Today

Despite the new luxury mindset and its implication for those of us in the sales industry, selling hasn't changed much in the past few decades, but the world sure has. Take a walk through the business section of your local bookstore or think back to the last training seminar you attended.

Chances are the material focused on skill sets, the individual tactics designed to help you prospect better, use technology efficiently or close more effectively. These are helpful and useful, but they're only half the picture when approaching the new luxury mindset. The other half, the more important half, is gaining a mental edge.

The goal of this book is to assist you in the strategy for developing and keeping that much needed mental advantage as you go out and actively target the new luxury mindset. More than other books on selling, this is not a book that simply encourages its readers.

My personal goal is to empower rather than encourage you by changing the way you think about selling, generally, and selling to the select, specifically. I don't want you to conform to the normal pattern of reading this book and filing it away. Read this book and *actually use* the enclosed plan to transform your thinking and, of course, your future successes.

This book is about selling to the new luxury mindset and releasing and maximizing your own potential to target and eventually harness this elusive but lucrative market. In order to be a successful select sales person, you must also maximize your personal potential. It is too difficult to thrive in sales without self-improvement. To succeed in sales today, it's not enough to know about your products and services. Superior knowledge helps, but to make it you must out-think your competition, and you must know yourself.

A few years ago, I read *Releasing Your Brakes* by Jim Neumann, who I consider to be one of the world's foremost authorities on human potential and achievement. Neumann looks at the mind as a car being driven by a person with one foot on the gas and one on the brake. In order to truly move through life, he explains, we need to get past our fear and remove our foot from the brake.

Everyone remembers his or her first car. Mine was a 1964 Rambler, with a push button gearshift and the leftovers of a tan paint job. It lacked power steering and power windows and in fact, had very little power at all.

But it did have one redeeming quality that made it an okay car for a teenager discovering life's adventures. The Rambler had an amazing ability for reaching top speeds (20 to 25 miles per hour) when coasting down a hill.

My Rambler was barely suited as a means of transportation. Sometimes it started, and sometimes it didn't. Approaching a stop sign was nothing short of having a death wish. With all its flaws, the Rambler gave me my first taste of freedom.

The car analogy to sales is a good one. The primary reason sales people fail is because we have one foot on the brake. With one foot on the gas and one on the brake, we are constantly starting and stopping. We never gain momentum; we never speed toward our goals. If we want to succeed and maximize our potential, we must accept fear and then take our foot off the brake.

The new luxury mindset isn't afraid to buy from us; we can't be afraid to sell to them.

### Let's Get Physical: Body Language, Then & Now

I can remember when I first started to understand the concept of successful selling. I was fresh out of school and had been on countless interviews. It seemed like I'd been everywhere – banks, ad agencies and other firms large and small – with no success. I didn't want anything to do with sales but I was running out of options. I figured that just about anyone could get a job selling. It would do until I could land what I then thought of as a real job.

My plan didn't turn out as I'd envisioned. I started sending out my resume and interviewing with sales managers but to no avail. Each interview seemed to start off well enough but would always end with those dreaded words: "We'll call you and let you know."

It wasn't until I met Bob Williams that things turned around for me. As the branch manager for Xerox in Memphis, he was responsible for hiring. Bob's corner office was large and imposing, with a sweeping view of the Memphis skyline. As we made our introductions, I took in the view, a reminder of his position.

We began with questions about my background and non-existent work experience. After 20 minutes, we'd covered the basics. He took a few notes, but it was obvious to me that we were just going through the motions – asking the standard questions and giving the stock answers. The Bob said, "Greg, why should I hire you?"

To my chagrin, he leaned back in his chair and looked out the window, seeming disinterested in my answer. I persevered and took a shot.

I leaned in, got Bob's attention, and said, "You should hire me because I know exactly when I lost you in this interview." Surprised, he again focused on me.

Then I said, "Now you're back. You see, Bob, I can tell from your body language when I say things that interest you. If you hire me, I'll do the same thing with your customers, and I'll be able to sell Xerox copiers."

Bob didn't speak for what seemed like an eternity. Finally, a smile crept onto his face and he asked, "How did you do that? How did you know?"

I explained that a book on body language had made me aware that people have physical reactions and expressions that mirror their thoughts, even though most of those thoughts are never expressed in words. People don't always say what they think, and I could tell that he was holding back.

Bob was clearly interested. "What did I do that tipped you off?" he asked.

I answered that when the interview began, he leaned forward and looked directly at me with his arms unfolded. He'd asked a lot of questions, and I was sure that he'd been interested in meeting me.

After we spoke a while, however, he'd leaned back in his chair. Not long after, he'd folded his arms and broken eye contact. I told him that I knew at that point that I needed to regain his interest and attention, or he would not hire me.

As I spoke, I could feel my confidence soar. Bob was not only a branch manager, he was successful. After a pause he said, "Welcome to Xerox."

That was my first lesson in sales. Learn new skills and techniques, always seek self-improvement, and find a way to succeed

Focus on the positive and what has worked for you.

where you had previously failed. How could I have known that reading a book on body language would some day help me get a great job. That book put me on the path to success.

At Xerox, I learned the basics of selling and how to manage my time and myself. From that experience, my career jumped to CBS, Warner Brothers, and today to a speaking, writing and consulting career. That book brought me to a place in my life where I am now my own boss.

My purpose with this book is to provide a launching pad or a jump-start to help you sell more and have a successful career. Along the way, I will share what I've learned and the things that have worked for me. If something in this book seems like it can work for you, use it.

Each of us must find what works for us. Learning what works for others is a good place to begin. Focus on the positive, what you think will work for you, and use it to achieve success.

**Memo From The Future:** Selling to the New Luxury Mindset

While many experts refer to these as uncertain times, what is certain is that we have more "rich" people than ever. According to the World Wealth Report, compiled by Merrill Lynch and Capgemini Consulting, wealthy individuals increased by over 7% in 2005. The number of high net worth individuals (HNWIs) — individuals with a net worth of at least U.S. $1 million, excluding their primary residence — grew by 7.3% to 8.3 million, a net increase of 600,000 worldwide.

North America led with a nearly 10% growth rate to 2.7 million HNWIs, surpassing the 2.6 million in Europe. Asia-Pacific's growth rate of over 8% — to 2.3 million HNWIs — was twice that of Europe.

The growth in this "new face in wealth" has impacted sales of luxury products from automobiles to real estate. Interestingly, the companies who have the most to gain have not invested in improving the sales methods of the people who interface most with this customer... their sales teams.

**The Wrong Approach for the Right Audience:** Targeting the New Luxury Mindset

It was December, a month where car sales are typically slower than the rest of the year. As I walked in to one of the top BMW dealers in the United States, I was introduced to "my" assigned sales rep.

We quickly went through the basics, briefly discussed the kind of car I was looking for and whether I had a trade-in.

That's where it began, the standard car salesman jargon and actions. "What do you want for your trade-in? What will it take to make a deal today? How can I earn your business today? And my favorite, "Can you hold on and let me get my manager before you go?"

As this story points out, even the more admired automobile companies fall drastically short in the development and training of their sales people. Why would a person sell a $100K+ automobile using the same tactics as a person selling a $20K car? Or why would sales people in high-end jewelry stores position "friendliness" as their only tactic?

This concept of selling has been perpetuated in almost every area of the luxury market; from expensive homes to investments. It has even found its way into the luxury services arena, including cosmetic dentistry, plastic surgery, weight loss, vacations and more.

My four years of sales research, 20 years of Xerox/CBS sales training and presentations support this lack of sales acumen in each of the afore mentioned categories.

It's not that companies don't understand the value of developing their sales teams at this level; they are just plagued with a wealth of historically ineffective strategies. In this book we will offer a systematic approach to minimize the uncertainties of selling today in the luxury market and other markets as well.

To identify the thinking process and tactics that are most successful, we have constructed ongoing research that clearly identifies how the buyer thinks in today's market. Most training concepts focus on the selling techniques of top producers. But, we are more interested in the future as opposed to the history of the business.

From our research, we have identified the three top areas that will target and improve the thought processes of sales professionals and provide tools for more effective prospecting.

As you read, think of your mantra as "your past failures have nothing to do with your future." Think positively: "You can make it in sales." I openly announce that you can make it because I have never met a "Born Salesperson."

I know top salespeople in 31 cities where I have given speeches, and a person in each one of them learned how to become great in sales. What's key here is that *they are still learning*; still reading; listening to tapes; and still trying to improve.

The First Aptitude -- is the "willingness to pay the price." You will have to invest in yourself the same way you invested in this book. When you take your money and re-invest it in yourself, you become a business.

The Question is -- do you have the willingness to become a pro? The cost is high, but the return is even higher. Can you set a goal of becoming a pro and let nothing get in your way?

As I have worked in sales and in sales training, I have noticed something. I noticed that many of the so-called sales reps came to the meetings simply because their bosses insisted.

Here's a peek into how those sales losers think:

- **It won't be worth the effort.**
- **Why should I change?**
- **Why be uncomfortable building something new?**
- **I'm entitled to my leisure time.**
- **It won't work for me – it's not my style.**
- **It won't work in my business.**
- **Final cop out – I can work it out myself.**

# "Simply making consistent investments in our self-education and knowledge banks pays major dividends throughout our lives." Jim Rohn

Are you ready for a record-breaking sales career? Good, then let's get started learning the essentials. The strategies you are about to learn are essential for selling success in today's market. They include what I call *The 14 Proven Essentials for Selling to the New Luxury Mindset.*

So what are you waiting for?

The 1st Essential awaits…

essentials

## Selling Summary

**Your success is predictable in the Luxury Market. It requires however, a consistent regimen of sales education, skills practice and a higher level of knowledge about your customer.**

## The 1st Essential

Understanding the GIRI
Concept of Elite Prospecting

# The 1st Essential

## Understanding the GIRI Concept of Elite Prospecting

GIRI is an important part of Japanese social relationships. The word means "duty" or "obligation" arising from a social interaction with another person.

Despite the rapid change of Japanese life, ideas and society, the concept of "GIRI" has remained and still strongly governs Japanese social behavior. It is even now accepted as forming an important part of Japanese social relationships and is a perpetual theme in a variety of arts.

How does GIRI relate to the Luxury Selling Process? The higher you go up the economic ladder, the more the consumers depend on previous relationships. In most cases the wealthy would prefer not to buy from strangers. Interestingly, the majority of sales people still believe that the "cold call" from a stranger has a high probability of success.

Cold calling is a perfect example of *what doesn't work*. For many companies, cold calls or cold contacts are the preferred methods of generating new business for practically all salespeople.

Here are just a few of the reasons why cold calls don't work:

**1. Most salespeople have been trained superficially.**

**2. The effectiveness of cold calling was significantly reduced with the introduction of the Internet and its ease of information gathering.**

**3. Cold calling, of necessity, places the sales rep in a reduced position.**

**4. Cold calling only has a 17% success rate but consumes 70% of the average sales rep's schedule.**

**5. Cold calling destroys sales peoples' attitudes.**

Since 9/11, Y2K and the Iraq War, cold calling has experienced steady declines in success patterns. In spite of these facts, sales managers in nearly all companies continue to demand that salespeople spend their productive time cold calling instead of developing strategies that deliver consistent business.

It only takes a slight slowdown in sales before those familiar words "make more cold calls" and "you need to increase your activity" are heard from sales managers, regional directors and even presidents and CEOs.

On the other hand, the most dominant skill required for successful sales is prospecting. Any sales person who can prospect well is almost assured of success. In starting my sales career at Xerox, I had a chance to work with and observe one of their best sales people, Lewis Weiss.

The consistent sales success Lewis demonstrated was dominated by the concept of prospecting. If you applied percentages to his work-day, over half of his day was spent prospecting or taking care of current clients. As a result his sales were always in the top 20% of the branch. The key – his prospecting – was tied to developing relationships.

It has been my experience that to be successful in luxury and most other forms of sales, you must be successful in developing one-on-one relationships. Take it one step further, and look at all relationships as having "six degrees of separation." Simply put, we are all within six contacts of meeting anyone we want to work with.

Consequently, the basis for the most "effective selling" is a previous relationship and/or previous client success. Hence the foundation for building a sales network. It allows you to build a client base far more readily because you are more comfortable.

When you are more comfortable, your ability to become more aware increases. It is this awareness of opportunity that provides the opportunity to sell.

Look at prospecting like becoming a great trout fisherman. Traditionally speaking, trout are very clever and difficult to catch, therefore, they are prized. Sales leads and opportunities – particularly among the new luxury mindset – are as elusive as the trout.

For that reason alone, this process should be exciting. You need to think and base your actions on what will cause the fish to respond.

## Create a Proactive Approach

1.  Think rather than cold call – who do you want to do business with?

2.  Gain as much background information as you can on the potential client prior to any contact.

3.  Identify potential client needs and problems prior to any contact.

4.  Match client needs and ideals with your company's ability to fulfill those needs. Devise tools that will fit into the resolution of those needs.

5.  Initiate the first contact with someone whom you have an association with who can deliver to you the targeted account.

The key to this approach stems from overwhelming responses to our database.

More than 90% of those polled preferred to be approached by people affiliated with someone else they know on a personal level or have done business with. In the luxury arena, the focus has to be on *who you know and how good your customer service will be* for increasingly high net worth individuals.

The following process compares a cold contact vs. a GIRI approach. "A" is you. "B" is the client you want to do business with. "C" is a person that you know or a person you have done business with.

The key here is that almost everyone you know is a "C." They are either small "c's" (know only a few people) or capital "C's" (know tons of people).

**Create a proactive approach.**

The key is to look at everyone you know as a "C". Here's how the process would look:

### Cold Call Method

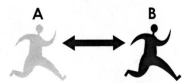

Potential Contact

**Odds:**
- 89% Failure Rate • 11% Success Rate
- Letter of Introduction • Dropping Off Literature

### GIRI Method

Potential Contact

**Odds:**
- 7% Failure Rate • 93% Success Rate • "C" Introduces
- The key to GIRI is "C's" ability and willingness to guarantee "A" to "B"

## The "Tie-In"

Under the GIRI method, when a person with credibility ("C") guarantees the sales person, it is simply an Indebtedness Introduction.

You have now created third party credibility, i.e., borrowing the credibility of "C" with decision maker "B". This action "ties" you into the potential client with the same connection you spent days, months, and years developing with person "C".

The critical questions a marketer needs to ask include:

- **How do you build or bring more of your contacts into your vision, your ideals?**
- **Who are my top 6 targeted accounts?**
- **How can I help my "C's" narrow the field of their contacts?**

In addition, the majority of their internal dialogue should continually ask, *"What company/client do I want to work with – who do I know that may also know them? What companies have I had the most success with – who might they know? Who, like me, has the same challenges?"*

Your first action must be thinking rather picking up the phone to call a stranger.

## awareness

### Selling Summary

**When you are more comfortable with how you meet people, your awareness increases. It is this awareness that creates opportunity to provide additional strategies to sell the affluent client. You will shift from salesperson to "advisor" almost instantly.**

## The 2nd Essential

Proper Thought

# The 2nd Essential

## Proper Thought

No one has the right to expect sales without effort -- we have to earn our customers' investment in us by helping them reach their goals. Even television can improve selling, if we pay attention to it.

Here's what I mean: Recently I received a collector's box set of my favorite show, *Seinfeld*. As I watched "The Making Of" featurete, I learned that the show came out of a conversation with Larry David and Jerry Seinfeld making fun of actual situations. I also learned that *Seinfeld* broke every rule. David and Seinfeld pitched the show by explaining that their concept is about nothing, which later became an episode. Other life experiences also developed into episodes on *Seinfeld*.

What do *Seinfeld* and selling have in common? Television executives rush to produce hit television shows, to sell the public on the next great hit, while business executives rush to get products to market and sell them.

In the '70s, products were often tied to phrases such as "features rich." In the '80s, products were connected to benefits. Sales persons received little training. For example, I earned my selling stripes by working for Xerox and going through their patented system "Professional Selling Skills." Specifically, I attended courses like Telephonics, Effective Listening, Asking Questions and many more. At the time Xerox was regarded by many to be the leader in sales training and those lessons helped shape every success I've had in sales.

In the '90s, we experienced the best of times. I was living in Seattle at the time and witnessed many deals that were done on napkins, ideas funded without plans and as some got rich, many forgot how to sell. Then came Y2K fears, the Dot com crash, and a war, and the economy sputtered.

The alarm sounded, and selling became Business Development. Fear caused companies to worry about a future with diminishing sales revenue. As I worked with sales teams across the nation, I found that the lack of selling wasn't confined to Seattle. Many companies experienced a declining ability to sell.

Some businesses found themselves desperately short of revenue. This state of fear within those businesses resulted in taking shortcuts to selling. I think the most interesting thing about this is that both good times and bad times resulted in similar sales processes.

But different times, different economic conditions and different factors require us to respond differently. Instead of reacting, in sales we need to always be proactive, creative, innovative and productive because we understand our customer's wants and needs, which change as their business environments change.

Instead, we hurried and rushed to get new business. We played by the old rules without recognizing that our customers were playing by a different set of rules. Unfortunately, the scenario described above happens far too often. Most companies sell year after year, repeating the same mistakes, and not adapting to changing industries and business trends.

To avoid making similar mistakes when selling to the new luxury mindset, consider the following: It is how you think that results in success or failure. For example, I have been around sales professionals who were more skilled, more intelligent and more senior than I. Their inability to use those gifts, however, had more to do with their lack of thinking and planning than it did with their abilities.

**"When nothing seems to help, I go look at a stonecutter hammering away at his rock perhaps a hundred times without as much as crack showing in it. Yet at the hundred and first blow it will split in two, and I know it was not that blow that did it, but all that had gone before." Jacob Riis**

Instead of rushing out to make a sale, they should have done the following first:

They should have prepared their *week in advance*. It is essential to plan the week's activity, so the list goes into your subconscious mind and proper thoughts will happen during the course of normal activity.

With the experience of coaching sales reps at three successful sales organizations (Xerox, CBS and Warner Bros.), I found a common success thread: Those sales reps that prepared their week before it started experienced a greater degree of sales success.

## Build Your Confidence

How will you begin to effectively sell to the new luxury mindset? Selling to the luxury-inclined requires a more personal interaction, so the best place to start is with you. Start by creating more of a life roadmap with your personal goals; during tough times it's our goals that pull us along.

Learn the company by getting to know people, not company issues. The better your feeling about being part of a "team," the more your confidence will grow.

The new luxury mindset is all about quality, not quantity; so should your salesmanship be. Become an expert on company products *one at a time*. To attempt to learn many products at once will confuse you and tear down your esteem.

When you learn the products by becoming an expert on each product sequentially, you keep esteem at an all-time high.

When dealing with the luxury markets, it is of extreme importance to know the customer's vision better than your competition. And to know the answer to questions such as – "Where do you see yourself in three years?" Or "if we are successful, how will you be judged?" Questions of this nature demonstrate to the client that your efforts are geared to *help them* rather than just to *sell them*.

In 1937 there was a little known paper written called *Social Intelligence* [Social Participation and Social Intelligence, F. Stuart Chapin, *American Sociological Review*, Vol. 4, No. 2 (Apr., 1939), pp. 157-166]. The paper was the pre-cursor to Daniel Goldman's work on Emotional Intelligence. *Social Intelligence* discussed factors leading to success. Author F. Stuart Chapin claimed that success is guided empathy, observation of people patterns, and the determination of positive or negative emotion.

Forget cold calling. If you adapt just one idea from this book, it should be *stop cold calling today*. Why spend so much energy and time on a tactic that reaps such a small return on investment? Instead, reach out to the people you know who do business with you or who can help you contact others.

Why talk to strangers when you can talk to people you know? Employ the *Six Degrees of Separation Principle* that states that you are within six contacts of everyone. According to this theory, you know someone who can help you get a meeting with the president of a target account – or even the President of the United States.

Whether you are a sales person or a sales manager, everyone needs help to keep the focus on daily goals. The National Science Foundation states that the average person deals with 60,000 thoughts a day. About 90% of those thoughts are negative. To promote positive thinking, help your team see things differently.

This new vision will include things such as a new house, children's college education or retirement for mom and dad. Tie the things your team wants and needs to the numbers required to meet their sales goals and revenues. In every private meeting and every conversation make their vision the goal. By doing this, you and your team will achieve your sales revenue.

As you read this book, notice that we target actions that get results in today's market:
- **Proper mental focus**
- **Six Degrees of Separation Prospecting**
- **Using and managing positive thinking and a new vision**

To succeed, I recommend that you approach problems and challenges similarly to the biochemist, Szent-Gyorgyi. He believes that, "If we are faced with a problem, we approach it without

As you grow, you improve your ability to sell.

preconceived ideas and sentiments like fear, greed and hatred. We approach it with a cool head and collect data which we eventually try to fit together."

## Success Is in Our Minds

# "Ours is the age that is proud of machines that think and suspicious of men who try to." H. Mumford Jones

This book could be a turning point in your sales career as well as in your life. I want it to have that kind of impact. But to have impact, you have to participate. In every conference or seminar that I speak, people approach me afterward. One thing they say stands out above all else: It's not what I say; it's what they hear that matters.

The same principle works here. If you read and absorb small things you can have big results. I hope you read with the idea of learning and gaining from my experiences. Let's start by embracing the idea that everyone sells. I sell, you sell, the minister, the barber, the dentist, and even small children sell.

We only sell, however, to the level of our self-concept, self-awareness and self-esteem. As we grow and improve our self-esteem, we improve our ability to sell. It's confidence that sells, and that confidence causes us to ask the difficult questions. It causes us to keep going when a client says "no."

## Getting More...

Let's start by being aware that competition comes from inside us. Until we stare defeat in the face and improve ourselves on a personal level, we cannot achieve record-breaking success, nor can the people around us depend on our effectiveness. The largest, most lethal competitor lives inside us.

With the 60,000 thoughts per day cluttering our minds, we must find clarity and focus on our success and not on outside influences. If 90% of all thoughts are negative and we tell ourselves that we cannot do a specific task, we short-circuit our future by limiting positive thinking and by convincing ourselves that our past dictates and determines our future. Although psychologists tell us that our past is a predictor of our future, it need not *determine* that future. At the end of the day, we decide whether or not we succeed or fail.

When we engage in negative thinking and conversation, it blocks our paths to success. It's not that our competitors perform at such a high level; it's that we waste time thinking about them. We think they perform at a higher level, and we talk ourselves into believing it and surrender to the belief.

We remember the one or two advances the competition makes and negatively think that is how they perform 100% of the time. They don't.

Here's the truth: *a better sales person lives inside you, right now, today*. So, beginning right now, stand up, be positive, feel confident and assume your place in the office, your place in the nation and your place in the lives of your family. Get up and get going. You are on the path to success. Now begin the long race to the finish line with confidence that you will succeed. Success is in your mind, not in what others say or do.

It begins right here, right now. I want you to read and digest every element of this book.

Grab onto the ideas that you find lacking in your personal makeup. Then, one at a time, practice each area of this personal improvement curriculum until it becomes ingrained. Your goal is to become an expert at each of the new skill sets.

This is one of the more important lessons of selling. We must practice the skills we want over and over again. Every athlete becomes great by practice and repetition, then, under the pressure of competition, they simply follow through. My goal here is to help you follow through and do so properly. Follow through in a way that helps you to grow and become wildly successful selling to the new luxury mindset.

Remember, these are people who are either a.) successful or b.) buying your product to make themselves look or feel more successful. Success breeds success; if they are going to buy from you they have to believe in you – but that can only begin to happen when you start to believe in yourself.

I believe that the most exciting thing in life is to learn how to be better – how to do more and more of what we are capable of doing.

Ignore the voice of regret. Forget phrases such as "I should have said this" or "I should have done that." You waste energy and that results in nothing productive or good. Instead, let go of negativity and hold fast to positive thinking. It lightens your load and leads to success and pleasure.

## "You are the storyteller of your own life, and you can create your own legend or not." Isabel Allende

Every time I conduct training sessions, there are always one or two in the group who believe they have heard it all. I want them to ask themselves this question: "If I have heard it all, and learned everything the training has to offer, why aren't I more successful?"

The easy way out is to blame the training or the trainer, but the reality is that there is a great divide between what is heard and what we do with what we learned. No other person or no one trainer is responsible for your success. Only you can decide to be successful. And when you do, learning and re-learning will be one of the keys to your success.

There is a secret to digesting sales strategies and converting those strategies to success patterns, and here it is: The first part of the success strategy is repetition. From athletics to business, repetition increases retention and improves confidence.

Stop right now and think of one person you love and care about. Think how that person would benefit if you were more confident, more motivated and more in control of circumstances that have a negative effect on you and your loved ones. If you cannot think of another person, think about yourself?

Do you love yourself? Love is a great motivator and a strong reason for you to adapt success strategies. The monetary rewards and improved lifestyle you achieve aren't bad reasons to focus.

## Commission Beats Salary

Jim Rhon is one of my favorite speakers. One of the concepts Rhon believes in is that commission beats salary. Most people, however, fear the uncertainty of working on commission; they prefer the security of a regular, pre-determined paycheck to the opportunity provided by commissions.

Your wages, however, are not safe, not protected and not guaranteed. At any moment an employer can decide that you are no longer needed. The only protection you have is to be an outstanding performer. As such, you likely will never be fired. Now, if we agree on performance as a way of protecting your job, then let's take the next step.

Negotiate as much of a commission as possible, even at the risk of a lower salary or no salary at all. Remember, you only get to keep the job based on performance so make sure you are going to be paid for taking that risk. Take the risk, perform at an all-time high and make the largest amount of money possible.

An employer's money, you see, is made by taking a risk. Their risk is investing time and materials into a product, then selling that product and using the revenues to pay the people, who

make, sell and deliver the product. By accepting the same risk and taking more commission and less salary or no salary at all, you are going into business with your boss.

Then commit to being a professional and outperforming your boss's expectations. Your reward will eclipse any amount an employer would ever consider paying in salary. You want the big bucks? Be a skilled professional and demand to be paid for results.

**Insights into Success:** 5 Strategies for Selling to the New Luxury Mindset

We must look at selling as a part of life and a vital part of a better life, but before we go a step further, let me explain the basics of a successful selling career. Innovative selling, creativity, strategies and breakthroughs come most often from sources outside traditional business – look for answers in non-traditional places.

**To have longevity, here are five sales revelations:**

**Strategy # 1:**
**Relax enough to look at selling differently than your competition**
What's going on in leading edge companies that you can bring to your selling process? Your straight line to success comes from observation, adapting, testing and revising until you create your own personal sales process. That process will lead to a well-defined sales plan.

**Strategy # 2:**
**Grow to a point in sales where you will know intuitively what to do and say**
You arrive as a sales professional when you have an epiphany that points you to success by solving a client's problem. Recognize and accept that every client has a problem; that is why he or she is in the market to buy.

### Strategy # 3:
### Start today by seeing yourself as a person who helps rather than sells

Your success or failure mirrors your creativity; always look for the non-obvious solution. Success won't look like history; it will look like the future.

### Strategy # 4:
### Don't judge yourself by your past

Your history has nothing to do with your potential. Most sales people judge themselves on their failures, while the world judges them on their successes. Never get to a point in your career where you believe there is nothing more to learn. Your success comes from learning.

### Strategy # 5:
### "You only grow by the books you read and the people you meet," taken from a speech given by Lou Holtz, well-known football coach and motivational speaker.

If you understand and accept what you can gain, you will work harder. Using an imaginary sketchpad, draw the things you want most. Lay a foundation of clearly identifiable areas to improve your life.

What would you like to have, be or share? Is it a better car? Maybe you see your first home or a better home? Perhaps you see a picture of the future of those you love. A college fund for the kids, a retirement plan for mom and dad, or maybe a better life for you and your spouse.

These goals represent a clear picture of your life. If you can see why you are selling, you will prepare yourself to learn as you read this book. You learn in direct proportion to your need to learn. The need to learn is determined and supported by the personal benefits you anticipate. So anticipate.

Look forward to the things you want in your life. Feel the life you can create. If you thought that you could have things you wanted for your family or friends, would you learn better? For most of us the answer is yes. Complete control of your future lies in your hands, not the hands of others. By selling better you can do better, have more and share more.

method

## Selling Summary

**Your success in Luxury Markets will come from your ability to think; it is essential that we think in ways that allow constant upward mobility. It is not what we do that causes success; it is how we think.**

# The 3rd Essential

## Personal Magnetism

# The 3rd Essential

## Personal Magnetism

JFK had it. Ali had it. And there are others: Princess Di, Martin Luther King, Jr., George Clooney, Michael Jordan, etc. But what is it about them that made us buy into their philosophies or their personas? The 3rd Essential is how to create magnetism that attracts others to you.

Magnetism is always about self-confidence. Here is how I describe self-confidence: Self-confidence is feeling so good about yourself – there's enough left over to help someone.

### The First Product

Whether your company has 10 products to sell or 110, the first product is always you. Without the client's acceptance of you, the sales call goes nowhere. The 3rd Selling Essential is the Art of Attracting buyers and possible buyers.

You are now and will always be the "first product" clients decide to buy or not to buy. It is only after the client buys into you that they can begin to evaluate your product.

### Love Jon Richardson

Yes, I know – the name doesn't mean anything to you. But when I was in Junior High School, Jon Richardson was the guy I most wanted to be. Jon had a big brother who was a football star! Even more, Jon was smart, good looking, a football star in his own right, and he got along with everyone… including teachers. Here's the catch – Jon wasn't older than I. Jon was my age. I was puzzled at how someone so young could be so well liked and accepted.

At first I avoided Jon. I never said one word to him. Although we had classes together, I was just a little intimidated. That soon changed. After football season ended Jon came out for the basketball team. Now he was on my turf – I never played football but basketball was my love.

Soon Jon and I became friends, and I got to see what made people gravitate toward him. It turned out to be very basic things. Things that even I could do. As I would watch Jon interact with other classmates, he would:

- **Always open with a quick smile**
- **Many times, laugh out loud at their jokes and lean on them as he laughed**
- **With every conversation be totally focused on the person talking. It was almost like no one existed but the person he was talking to.**
- **Never say a harsh word about anyone**
- **(And this is a big one) -- Give everyone he approached or who approached him a high five, or a pound (fist clash) or put his arm around them. He would have some physical contact with them. And each time he would smile as big as daylight.**

Here's the amazing part: I started to mimic what Jon did and got the same result! I started with the quick smile with everyone. I used the high five, physical contact thing.

I even laughed at their corny jokes and leaned on them like I was running out of breath. I was stunned to see how differently people responded to me. It took me back to an old saying my Grandfather used, "When you look at yourself differently, others will too." Jon Richardson was the first of many people that I copied to improve my Personal Magnetism.

**"Before you can inspire with emotion, you must be swamped with it yourself. Before you can move their tears, your own must flow. To convince them, you must yourself believe." Winston Churchill**

### What Causes Magnetism?

Magnetism is a result of various emotional connections. Upon hearing your voice or seeing you, people start deciding if they like you. Experts have debated the issue for years of how quick or how long it takes to create magnetism. What has not been an issue is the idea that a person can learn the principles of developing magnetism. Let me say it another way in case you were drifting: *You can actually do specific things to improve your ability to build rapport and increase magnetism!*

To properly exhibit magnetism, there some basic thought processes we need to incorporate:

- **We teach people to accept us or not.**
- **Positive or negative energy creates the same.**
- **Enthusiasm and happiness breed the same.**
- **We sell with images, not words.**
- **Fear blocks potential.**
- **What people most remember is how you make them feel.**
- **We are all connected.**

These are the foundations for building an ability to attract people. They are the foundations for creating Magnetism. Let's take a look at each of these ideas. First, we teach people to accept us or push us away. In the first few seconds of each interaction we have, the person meeting us starts to make decisions about us.

Interestingly, we have far more control over the outcome than we may think. For example, your confidence assures people that previous success has contributed to your apparent "glow." And if you add things like a positive attitude, humor and maybe an item you have in common – your stock quickly soars.

Here's how those concepts may appear. When a client puts forth a particular behavior, be it positive or negative, your reaction affirms or disallows future actions. When we have the ability to "illuminate" ourselves, it becomes easier to attract people to us. In that process it becomes easier for clients to become attracted to us.

## People Bonding With People

When we meet a new person, we have a precious few seconds to attract or repel them. Certainly there are basics that we must consider, such as eye contact, smiles, body language, etc.

The one skill I have witnessed to be a savior if all else fails, however, is the art of conversation. Specifically, if you get a new contact and want to make a solid impression, I suggest you talk less and listen more. The percentages should come close to 75% to 25%. That's 75% listening and 25% talking.

## Speaker Magnets

I have always felt that the real way to build rapport is through conversation. This is a skill, a learned behavior that we must work on continuously to improve. What most people overlook is that being a good conversationalist is more about listening and remembering than about talking. The goal should be to develop a conversation where the other person talks about their interests.

With every conversation, look for common ground. The moment you can connect on a hobby, movie, book, etc., the conversation takes off to a higher dimension. It doesn't have to be life changing; you can start rapport with small things such as a statement rather than a question.

When you make a statement, it assumes that you have moved past awkwardness. Notice that friends often start their conversations with statements rather than questions.

Such as:

- **"Don't know if you heard, but our flight has been delayed due to an improper door part!"**
- **"It's okay if you sit here, but you've got to agree not to discuss the heat!"**

Now, if the boldness of making statements is out of your comfort zone, you can also use questions for similar results. Many people feel that questions are easier. Careful here, we only want to ask questions that are the Wh's.

Those are the questions that start with words like What, Where, When, Who or Why. In each case ask these questions in a way that allows the person to talk past a basic yes or no answer. When you ask a "Wh" question, the listener has to talk more.

Let's look at asking questions in a way that ties in more personal elements:

1. **Ask the person "Where are you from originally?" This question automatically gives you an advantage. You are perceived as someone who was observant enough to see something in them.**

2. **Ask, "Why did you get into this profession?" Be prepared for the whirlwind tour here. Most people can talk for hours about this one.**

3. **I want to be gentle here … ask about family or pets. Phrasing might include a question like, "So how does family figure into this busy schedule of yours?"**

Notice the progression here. We start with very basic but intriguing openings. We allow them to become more comfortable with them and us. Next, we make a turn from common ground things to questions that allow open dialogue. And, finally, we get more personal information.

This process would not work if you started by asking about more personal things right away; it's too abrupt, particularly for the more sophisticated luxury market. By allowing them to talk about non-threatening things, however, we are allowed to ask more and more personal things.

In the end, we are all closer to the people we share our most personal thoughts with. Remember three more things:

- **MAKE – people feel important**
- **ASK – for what you want**
- **LISTEN – more and talk less**

The great differentiator is how you make people feel!

## The Second Movement

Who is actually in sales?

In short: everyone!

Everyone is in the business of selling. Let's just cut to the chase. I said this earlier, and I will say it again, everyone sells. If you are in, about to be in, or have been in any situation that requires the help of another person… you are in the profession of selling. Long gone are the days of force and dictatorship.

We depend more today on the power of persuasion than ever before. There are small favors, big commitments, jobs, marriages, business deals and the list goes on. Any gentleman reading this book needs to stop and go back a few years.

If you are married, you sold that deal! Very few women see men walking down a crowded street and shout to the top of their lungs, "Look at that hunk of man candy. I have just got to figure out a way to breed with him!"

No, in the large majority of marriages, men pursue their future mates with basic dating rituals. Those tactics are just another form of selling. Nevertheless, the overriding fact is that we must sell – no longer can we use force as a method of persuasion. I am almost sure the "force" thing went out with hula-hoops. So let's start the selling process here by attracting people to us.

Let's look at *Personal Magnetism* in its most basic form:

- **The Eyes Have It:** Every conversation you have with someone, you should focus on spending time in their eyes. Especially when another person tries to interrupt the conversation. If and when that happens, keep your eyes focused on the person you are talking to. This same gesture tells them how important they are. And, in many cases, focused eye contact promotes the idea that you genuinely like them.

- **Style:** I have always been a big believer in "packaging." How you dress says something about you before you can open your mouth. I recommend 1.) Always be at or above the dress level of your client. (No jeans if they are wearing slacks or a dress) and 2.) Try and find something that can be a conversation piece. It can be anything from cuff links to earrings, from a style of dress to a bachelor's bow. If you have some interest in this one, try old movies. In many cases you will find the elements of style buried in screen legends like Cary Grant, Marilyn Monroe, Fred Astaire and others. One of my favorite movies is *An Affair To Remember*, starring Cary Grant. In almost every frame of this movie Cary Grant is telling men how they should dress.

- **Language:** As long as I can remember, people who had a command of the English language have been memorable. Sometimes it's the way you organize words or sometimes it's the use of little-used words that convey bigger meanings. But a wordsmith will always be remembered. One way to be remembered with words is to use metaphors to describe where you want the listener to go. Martin Luther King, Jr. was the master of metaphors. I can still remember speeches where he created a visual by comparing something I was familiar with to his topic. Phrases such as, "it's like" or "similar to" takes the listener to place where they can weave your words into thoughts.

- **Humor:** One of the more powerful ways of attracting people is with humor. Careful here, I'm not saying tell jokes, but I *am* saying that developing a keen sense of what is funny can be disarming and attractive at the same time. If you have never been good at being funny, I would suggest you study what makes people laugh. When you find something that works, remember it. If you are reading a book and a funny story comes out of it, keep the story and personalize it to a situation that comes up. Go to comedy clubs and watch both the comic and the audience... then remember what works. There are two kinds of comics. One is the natural comedian; that would be someone like David Letterman. It's not that the monologue is that funny, it's that his interaction with the guests is funny. The second kind of comic is what I call the learned comic, which would be Jerry Seinfeld. He is known in comedic circles to be one of the best writers in the business. Chris Rock said once that Jerry's advantage is that he knows how to make something by using it, "right there!" In other words, Jerry not only uses words but he is keen enough to use placement to get a laugh. Lastly, Jerry is known to keep a pad and a pen by his bed. He is prepared at all times so when an idea hits him, he writes it down and uses it in his standup. I saw Jerry Seinfeld at least four times when he was just starting out. I saw him use the same jokes, verbatim, again and again. Whether you are born with it or you learn it... use humor to attract.

- **Let me end with the biggest attraction of all: Helping not selling.** The moment a person sees that you are honestly trying to help them – they are attracted to you. All sales, therefore, should be an effort to help. Help your client get more revenue. Help them save money. Help them better utilize their employees. Or help them become a success at their vision. The moment you go from selling to helping, you cross the bridge into professionalism.

# "A year from now you may wish you had started today."
# Karen Lamb

### First, Get the Job

Now let's use your magnetism to get the job you want. Whether the job is in your present company or a new one, your first steps include preparation to get the job that you want. Study the industries that spark your interest. Is it broadcast sales, pharmaceutical, real estate or, in the case of the new luxury mindset, maybe it's the marketing of private jets? What are the things you would do for fun, as hobbies? What interests you most? I believe that a successful career decision is partly about money, but mostly about the way you live your life; the way you help others and the personal joy that you experience.

Once you decide on an industry, determine its category leader. Put that company in your sites. Let's say the industry you select is luxury apparel. Who's at the top or who is an "up and comer"? Maybe it's St. John's or Armani, or it could be a tested product such as Ralph Lauren. Research and find a way to get in the door (perhaps using Six Degrees of Separation, discussed in Chapter 6).

Set up an interview and then turn your attention to preparation and follow-up. Before the interview, learn as much as you can about the company.

Explore the company's web site, its brochures, annual reports, news articles and whatever you can find. Talk to friends, employees and the competition. Learn what others think and say about your future employer.

Create a one-page killer resume. Highlight your successes. Focus on measurable results. For example, instead of saying something like, "I lead the team in sales," give specific goals and percentages. It should read something like this: "I ended the year at 160% of my goal and 63% better than the next best sales person."

Talk and write about the company. For example, point specifically to the job you want within the company and detail how your skills are perfect for a position with the company. Don't forget to write about why you want to work with that company and why you are a good fit.

Here are other tips:

- **Create a selling notebook. Include any item that helps showcase you as a sure bet. Include:**
  - **Letters of recommendation**
  - **Memos on past sales success**
  - *Specific awards*
  - **And, above all, support documentation that describes your volunteer and charitable work**

Place volunteer and charity work documents after your business success letters. Be specific about the help you have provided charities and how positive you felt in doing so.

Finally, you need a closing action and statement. Here's an example of one that has worked for me. Create a mock news story with a headline such as "Winston Joins XYZ, Inc." Insert a business headshot of yourself along with a story of your pending success.

Doing something unexpected shows you as a creative thinker and powerful addition to the team. In addition, having fun with the interview exudes confidence.

Before the interview you must create an interactive presentation. Search for information on the person interviewing you. Begin the interview with something about the interviewer. Here's an example: "Mary, how does a person come from sales assistant to Sales Manager in just three years?"

Doing this shows the interviewer that you respect them, that you have done your homework, and that you are on top of your game.

When the interviewer answers the question, listen intently. Their answer might be the key to helping you get the job. In most cases, you will hear the important items that most sales people miss. Listen and then take out your Selling Notebook.

Starting with your resume, show how your career is similar to the interviewer's. That creates a connection. Be careful not to go too far with this.

Give three or fewer selling statements that set the way for you to say, "Can you see how my success in selling bonus offers is the same as when you sold supply specials?" Make sure the interview is an exchange of information. If at all possible, ask questions and reduce the amount of time you talk. The more they talk, the better your position. As the conversation continues, you will stand out as the candidate who established rapport, the one who had that special something, the one who had "IT".

Now you put a ribbon on the package and wrap up the job. Review all the important points on which you connected;. the points you had in common with the interviewer. Then present the newspaper story. And conclude by asking, "What do we need to do to make this news story a reality?"

## Presentation

A big part of winning in sales is the presentation. We begin every presentation by presenting according to the needs of the clients. Clients have three areas of concern that we can call: help, time and pressure.

- **Help:** Clients are interested in whether or not you can **help** them and make them look good. They drift in and out of the conversation. They only want to know if your product can help them personally or help their company, so focus on specific solutions that meet their wants and needs, not the features of your product.

- **Time:** Once they believe that you can help them, they want to know when. If you can help but can't do it within the client's *time* frame, then you can't help them. To close the

Professionally showcase your work for a sure bet.

sale, you need to provide a solution within the client's time frame.

- **Pressure:** Client's fear closing. They worry about making a mistake. You must make them feel as if they are in control of the sales process. The client must believe they are buying your solution, instead of feeling that they are being sold; eliminate the *pressure* to make the sale.

Start with an opening statement that touches on each one of the client's concerns. Share how you can help, the time it will take to provide the solution, and your company's ability to keep their promises and meet their deadlines. If you have an example of a similar situation, share it.

An opening statement might sound like this: "Bob, thanks for the time today. Before I got here I did some research you might find interesting. I discovered that we have helped 17 companies the same size and scope of yours.

We were able to help them within three days. Today, I want to tell you how we partnered with them and then you make the call about whether or not we take the next step in doing business. Does that seem fair?"

At this point, the client is prepared to listen. If you start a presentation without building this foundation, clients might not hear much of what you have to say. Instead of listening, the client is wondering whether or not you can help.

In today's selling environment, clients – particularly those with the new luxury mindset – don't want to be sold, they want to buy. Your job is to move from selling to allowing the client to buy.

Here are more tips to improve presentations:

- **The Package:** Your tone of voice is central to making the client feel comfortable. Sound friendly but professional.

Interaction is key. Never make more than four statements without keeping the client on track with attention getting phrases such as, "Do we agree with this?" or "Tell me how this would be used." Use words that stir emotion, such as "winning," "worry-free" and "solvable". Mix in success phrases such as, "success," "successful," "increased productivity," "decreased costs," "increased revenues" and "market-leader".

- **Pleasure**: Listen carefully to the client's problem. Most sales close because they solve a problem. Without a problem, the client doesn't need you. Once you determine the problem, improve the client's life by solving the problem. The real accelerator in sales is the promise of a better future. Nothing you can demonstrate can surpass what the client dreams. You only have to sell the promise of their dream.

- **Experience**: Sell the experiences of other clients. If you truly want to touch your luxury client's heart and mind, share success stories. Show evidence of how you solved problems of similar clients with similar wants and needs. That provides the client with a vision of success.

- **Key Words:** The new luxury mindset wants to luxuriate in their decisions; they want word pictures brought to life that appeal to their suddenly sumptuous sensibilities. For this audience in particular, the right words draw pictures for the client. Pictures create feelings and thoughts. The power of pictures stir emotions in a client like no brochure or demonstration can.

- **Order**: First isn't always best, particularly when it comes to the luxury market. Make every effort to present *last*. If there are other companies vying for the client's business, ask the order of presentation. If you go last, the client hears the same things over and over again. That makes your job easier. Because you come in, set the presentation to the side, and instead of talking about how great your product is, you discuss your client's want and needs. The conversation is about your client, not your product. Remember, people buy people FIRST; the purchase of products and services comes after they buy you.

The ideas we just laid out are useful with clients and in job interviews. Leave your baggage behind. Focus completely on the client or the interviewer, not on yourself.

## command

### Selling Summary

**We must look at the total package in the Luxury Market to create Personal Magnetism. It begins with our style of dress, our physical movement and continues to our ability to engage the client emotionally. It is critical that the client buys you first. Remember they have access to the product you sell through many sources.**

## The 4th Essential
Positive Internal Dialogue

# The 4th Essential

# Positive Internal Dialogue

The new luxury mindset is built on belief. Fancy cars denote good jobs, fancier houses convey prosperity and success, fancy clothes culminate in all of the above.

These are people who want to focus on the positive in their own lives, and hence respond more favorably to salespeople who approach them with confidence, poise and positivity.

So as the number of messages increase in our lives, it becomes more and more important to filter out the ones that are self-destructive. With an average of 50,000 thoughts a day, yours is the voice you hear most. Consequently, *you are who you believe you are!* You are as good or as bad as you think you are. The 4th Essential guides us toward better ways to create positive self-talk.

As James Allen, author of *The Path to Prosperity*, once said, "Man is made or unmade by himself; in the armory of thought he forges the weapons by which he destroys himself; he also fashions the tools with which he builds for himself heavenly mansions of joy and strength and peace.

By the right choice and true application of thought, man ascends to the Divine Perfection; by the abuse and wrong application of thought, he descends below the level of the beast. Between these two extremes are all the grades of character, and man is their maker and master."

## "The best captain does not plunge headlong, nor is the best soldier a fellow hot to fight. The greatest victor wins without a battle." Lao Tzu

### Overcoming Fear

Fear seems to be a natural reaction in salespeople. It was in me. Somehow I felt afraid when I began my sales career. There was always a mixture of emotions. I felt like I was imposing. I felt like I was somehow tricking potential customers. It didn't matter the product. I felt that people were doing me a favor if they bought it.

As a child I sold newspapers on a street corner. I remember a hot summer evening standing near a traffic light. As shiny late-model cars filled with executives and families passed me going home, I would hold up the latest edition and shout, "Democrat! Get your evening Democrat here!"

When the cars stopped for the traffic light, I walked down the line of cars holding up a copy of the paper, too nervous to say anything. I would just show the paper.

When the light changed, my confidence came back and I would bellow as loud as I could, "Democrat! Get your evening Democrat here!" Selling newspapers was my first exposure to sales. For the life of me, I couldn't understand why rich people needed a newspaper or why they needed me to sell it to them.

So there I was, standing on my favorite newspaper corner, right across from the doughnut shop. I could smell the fresh doughnut dough. Soon, I knew that I could finish selling papers and run across the street for my favorite doughnut, chocolate-filled glazed. Oh, I could just feel the chocolate oozing out as I took my first bite. One or two more bites, and I'd wash it down with milk so cold it would cause brain-freeze.

As I snapped back to reality, I saw that the light had turned red, and one of the rich people was talking to me as he rolled down the window of his air-conditioned car. I looked at him with that non-blinking, reptilian-like stare, and he shouted again over the noise of traffic, "HEY KID ... DO YOU HAVE AN EXTRA?"

"No," I said. He looked at me in disbelief.

Then the light changed, and he drove off.

I stood there motionless. *Oh my God*, I thought. *He wanted a paper*. I was so nervous around people and selling that my brain shut down. I had a stack of newspapers. I certainly knew what the word "extra" meant, but fear caused my doughnut-focused mind to shut down. While it may have appeared that I functioned on the outside, my inside mechanisms had stalled. Fear is the greatest enemy of selling professionals. It holds us back, it slows us down and it causes us to miss life's greatest opportunities.

Before there can be consistent, reliable growth in *the selling process*, you first have to have consistent, reliable growth *as a person*. Fear stifles our talent. It causes us not to do what we know we can. Fear blocks our progress.

**The First Movement:** Self Development

Most of what causes us to improve is centered within human development. Nowhere is this more evident than the recent surge in interest of Emotional Intelligence. Emotional Intelligence has become a hot topic in corporate America.

When the *Harvard Business Review* published an article on the topic five years ago, it attracted a higher percentage of readers than any other article published in the last 40 years. So impressed was the CEO of Johnson & Johnson that he had 400 copies sent to his company's top executives.

Emotional Intelligence got its start in the early 1930s. The team of Salovey and Mayer coined the term emotional intelligence in 1990. They described emotional intelligence as "a form of social intelligence that involves the ability to monitor one's own and others' feelings and emotions, to discriminate among them, and to use this information to guide one's thinking and action."

One study revealed that when a group of people saw an upsetting film, those who scored high on emotional clarity (the ability to identify and give a name to the mood that is being experienced) recovered more quickly.

In another study, individuals who scored higher in the ability to perceive accurately, understand and appraise others' emotions were better able to respond flexibly to changes in their social environments and build supportive relationships.

This ability is a tremendous benefit in the selling process. Those who demonstrate social intelligence will have an appreciably higher percentage of selling success. Being able to react positively in the face of a difficult challenge, to interact well with peers and to get others to react with good feelings and cooperation becomes the basis for growth within most social groups, and that is especially true in sales.

So how do the findings in Emotional Intelligence studies affect the selling process?

Leadership Selling is a form of leadership. If your ability is improved to better handle the difficulties of selling, you become a better leader. More importantly, you can better lead your client to appropriate decisions.

## H.A.B.E.: The 90% Factor

I've said this before but my introduction to major selling was at the direction of the Xerox Corporation. I was instructed by the best, who were in turn armed with the most effective and important sales information available. Therefore, it seems odd that my most rewarding lesson on sales did not come from Xerox! That lesson revolved around the concept of H.A.B.E. or:

- **H** = **Habits**
- **A** = **Attitude**
- **B** = **Beliefs**
- **E** = **Expectations**

Here's how it works:

- **Habits:** Your *Habits* become nothing more than an automatic function. Habits are a form of pre-conditioning. My question is a simple one. What would change in your life if you changed your pre-conditioning to a more positive, upbeat and "I Can" function?

- **Attitude:** The answer is *Attitude*. It's the first change you will see when you choose more positive preconditioning. Your improved attitude will become the emotional side of those habits. You start to feel as if you can, and that attitude will change every social interaction you have.

- **Beliefs:** Next, you will begin to believe more in your self, hence your *Beliefs* will improve. Things that have been off limits will seem attainable now. You will approach thinking and doing in a different manner. You will believe and as you believe, your actions will follow. It's not one or two things in life that are governed by belief; everything and everyone are tied to belief. With beliefs in tow we can now expect more of ourselves.

- **Expectations:** *Expectations* are a combination of Habits, Attitude and Belief. We develop patterns with proper thought that help us to expect more of ourselves. And when we "expect" we receive just like when we predict, "lack of" or "failure" we get the same. Smarter people than I support this kind of thinking.

Take Dr. Albert Bandura, a leading cognitive theory psychologist and researcher a Stanford University. Dr. Bandura and other prominent cognitive theorists have conducted extensive research showing that humans can drastically impact their sense of well-being and optimism, career options and confidence levels.

The research supports a simple formula: Behavior = Heredity + Environment. While you can't change heredity, you can start today to change environment. The environment you spend most of your time in is your largest influence.

Let's start immediately: become your own authority and make your authority the most positive, habit forming, attitudinal, belief based, life expectant outlook you can visualize.

## "If You Want to Be Successful, *Don't Watch 60 Minutes!*"

Xerox rated all sales people on a Stack Ranking System. Tom Carr was the leading sales person in the Memphis branch. If you made it to 100%, you were a celebrated sales rep with the possibility of receiving an award at the end of the year. At 150%, Tom was held in high regard.

At my request, Tom gave me my first lesson in creating solid, long-lasting sales success. Tom's premise was that consistent, good sales habits would provide consistent sales success. In my first book, *When Life is a Barbed Wire Fence*, I described Tom's philosophy. Tom explained that while the rest of the sales team watched *60 Minutes* every Sunday evening, he prepared his sales strategy for the following week.

"Greg, I take out a sheet of paper and list every client I plan to see that week," he explained. "On the left side of the client's name I write down how much money I will make if I am successful with them. On the right side of the client's name I write how much money the client will save or how much they make with increased productivity if I help them.

The left side of the page gives me confidence; the right side of the page gives me courage. In most cases these clients come off that sheet of paper and go into my sub-conscience and I begin to think of what I will say long before I am in their presence. If you want to be successful, don't watch *60 Minutes*."

Tom had given me the first clue to creating habits that would produce sales success. Good habits build a strong foundation for sales success. Because my habits improved, I experienced an up tick in my attitude. I quickly became more confident, more aggressive and happier.

Perhaps it was because I had a clear idea of where I was going and what I was doing everyday. Or maybe it was because planning allowed me the time to practice what I was going to talk to the client about. The end result was that my clients saw an attitude that was so engaging that it gave each client more confidence in me.

As my attitude became more and more aligned with my sales

approach, my sales volume increased. By year's end, I received an award for sales performance. The award was called the "Super Rookie of the Year Award."

As my manager called me to the front to receive the award he made a startling announcement. "Greg, the average number of machines sold was 3.5 per month. You, Super Rookie, have averaged 7 machines per month."

Walking back to my seat I had one recurring thought: I'm twice as good as those other guys. What I was really saying to myself was that my beliefs about my ability were improving. And as my confidence grew, so did my sales success. The connection between belief and action was becoming more and more real to me.

From that day forward, when I wrote my weekly action plan I started with this statement at the top of the page, 2X as Good. In other words, "I'm going to be twice as good as those guys," was my consuming thought.

Xerox awarded me a territory and by the end of the second year I was on my way to record-breaking performance. My stack rankings hit an all-time high of 1003%. Let me be clear here.

While I certainly enjoyed the notoriety of being a top rated sales person, the lesson I learned was that my history had nothing to do with my potential. And just as I sold in other reps territory and got no credit, there were people who sold in my territories and got no credit.

From the receptionist to accounting to reps who came before me, we sell together. Selling has to be a community event.

Our background, race, sex, height, weight and hair color have little to do with rapid growth in sales. You want to sell more, have more, and share more with the ones you love? Read on.

## Rejection

One of life's greatest fears is rejection. Is it possible that your fear originates because you do not understand your product and the needs of your clients? Do you think of yourself as a resource for providing solutions? One clear message I received from Tom Carr was his view on *helping versus selling*. If you provide solutions instead of selling products, I believe your fear will lessen or disappear.

The first step in attacking fear is to define the problem. We sales professionals work every day with impaired vision. Shaped by sales lessons that were incorrectly taught, we go out daily using skills that don't work. That is part of the problem. A larger part of the problem, however, lies in the way we think and how we think about ourselves.

Beliefs determine behavior, which determines performance. If you want to change results, start with your beliefs.

Choose thoughts that contribute to your goals.

Believe in yourself and think positive thoughts.

**"The greatest discovery of my generation is that human beings, by changing the inner attitudes of their minds, can change the outer aspects of their lives . . . It is too bad that more people will not accept this tremendous discovery and begin living it."
William James**

**Your Journal:** The Best Book You Ever Read

One of the most effective ways to overcome fear and improve results is a daily journal. The premise is simple; most of what we learn, read and hear in life is negative. So we end up with negative thought process.

Keeping a journal changes negative factors into positive thinking. At the end of the day, write a short review of your day, next write three positive things that happened to you. Underneath those, write a positive goal for the following day.

How does this work? When you write down the three positive things you clear your mind of negative thought and instead focus on positive thinking. When you write down a goal for the following day, you create positive anticipation. Anticipation provides focus and doesn't allow your mind to slip back into negative thinking.

In much the same way when kids experience this every year around Christmas time. You now have something to look forward to, like a kid on Christmas morning. When you write a goal for yourself, your senses are heightened with anticipation.

To increase the effective use of your journal, frequently take time to read your writing from an earlier time. What you'll see is page after page filled with nothing but positive thought. And every word written and every message is a positive thought about you. This may be the best book you ever read:

## Today

## 3 Good Things

## Goals

The major difference between having and not having a plan is called efficacy. Efficacy means that you have the ability to cause something to happen. If you want to strike a goal, be prepared to cause things to happen in your life that benefit you and those around you. Nothing good happens in a day. But if you think positively, put positive thoughts in your journal, and plan daily, you can find the pot of gold at the end of the rainbow.

## Tell Yourself Good Things

My favorite sports hero is Muhammad Ali. Ali talked to himself. In the movie, *King of Kings*, there's a film clip that dramatizes the power that comes from talking to yourself.

It shows Ali speaking quietly to keep himself motivated. No one but Ali knew what he was saying. But whatever he was saying, it took him to the highest level of his career.

Keep in mind that every thought brings with it a physiological action, sometimes voluntary, sometimes involuntary. With all the thoughts we have each day, it only makes sense that we train ourselves to think in positive and powerful ways. We will have uncertainty and setbacks; they are part of all things new. Nevertheless, your positive internal dialogue, the way you talk to yourself, can get you to a level where setbacks won't bother you.

## Success Talk

The statements below come in two forms: failure talk and success talk. In each give and take, the sentence in bold type is failure talk; the sentence in italics is success talk. Notice how no matter how negative the failure talk may sound, the success talk always has an answer!

Here are examples of positive self-talk:

- "There will be problems."

"I know, and I will deal with them."

- "You may not succeed."

"Maybe not at first, but I'll stay on course."

- "People will reject you."

"We don't always get what we want on the first try, but I have to continue asking."

- "Are you really worth it and capable of it?"

"Yes I am. And the more I try the more capable I become."

forward

## Selling Summary

A great portion of effective selling to affluent customers is a positive view of ourselves. Selling professionals in Luxury Markets have to plan and constantly cultivate a higher than average positive outlook.

## The 5th Essential

The Time to Sell

# The 5th Essential

## The Time to Sell

"The new idea of selling: To undo some of the incorrect methods of past sales training done by the old ideas of selling."

**Greg Winston**

The great equalizer of success is the proper use of time. Even if you are expert at every sales skill in the world, you must conserve your time in a way that allows you to accomplish growth at "superstar" levels.

What does it mean to be a superstar? Your client knows. Those who worship at the altar of the new luxury mindset are either legitimate superstars in their own respective fields or want to look, feel and act like superstars, hence their need for whatever luxury product you're currently selling.

In short, these are risk takers, people who are not concerned with the mundane daily tasks but instead focus on the "I want it all, I want it now" mentality. Fearless, cocky, brave and daring, they expect just as much from their salesperson.

English essayist Sydney Smith once said, "A great deal of talent is lost in the world for want of a little courage. Every day sends to their graves obscure men whom timidity prevented from making a first effort; who, if they could have been induced to begin, would in all probability have gone great lengths in the career of fame. The fact is, that to do anything in the world worth doing, we must not stand back shivering and thinking of the cold and danger, but jump in and scramble through as well as we can. It will not do to be perpetually calculating risks and adjusting nice chances."

The idea of conserving and using time wisely never enters into most sales. Do you know how most people get started in sales? Sales people often start with a Bachelor of Arts degree. Unable to find a job in their degree of study, they take a sales job. They receive little or no proper training and are then thrown to the wolves to eat or be eaten.

So how can sales professionals improve and access more and more of their true potential? The sales people I know ask, "How can I become better in sales? Where can I learn more? What book should I read? How can I become better if I am selling in the worst possible economy?"

As I've said before, you improve in sales to the degree that you improve personally. The critical element is time. We must learn to use our time wisely in order to improve. The most important factor in time management is *your vision of the future*.

When you decide where you want to go and what you want to do with your life, you begin to dwell on positive thoughts of the future. Your focus on the future affects everything you do. And you begin to evaluate your progress by asking the right question: "Is what I'm doing right now helping me to achieve my goals."

## Don't "Find" Time You Don't Have, Manage the Time You Do

The biggest thing I have learned about managing time is, "It's not what happens between 8 and 5 that makes you successful. It's what happens *before 8 and after 5!*" Mediocre sales people put in their eight hours and race elsewhere: home, the bar, the coffee shop, the bookstore, the gym, the movie theater, whatever.

Superstar sellers know that preparation is key, and you can't prepare for what you're doing while you're actually doing it, so I recommend that you plan ahead the day/night before. With un-structured time it is important to keep your creative juices flow-ing so schedule that as well.

Set a specific deadline for tasks or items in your action fold-er. List items and deadlines on one master calendar and post it prominently. Color-code high-priority items, deadlines and fol-low-ups.

Once each week, let concerned parties know the status of spe-cific tasks. And follow these high-priority tips to appeal to the new luxury mindset:

- **Work effectively with others:** One of the most successful strategies you can employ is to contribute to the self-esteem of everyone around you: clients, vendors, colleagues, family members, and strangers. Cooperation builds relationships; competition erodes them. Share what you have and what you know; it will come back to you 10 times over. Express gratitude for what others share with you. Appreciate their talents, skills and accomplishments.

- **Improve your phone skills:** Your tone of voice contributes toward a successful telephone call. Most of us have a tendency to use what's known as a "business voice" when speaking to potential clients. It is slightly formal and tends to lack warmth. Instead, become accustomed to speaking in the same tone of voice you use with friends. It will make you and your client feel relaxed and comfortable. The key here is to practice with friends, then transfer those learned skills to your work.

- **Listen actively:** Listen actively to everyone speaking with you. If you have trouble concentrating, paraphrase each sentence spoken. Don't let yourself drift. Listen for tone of voice, pauses, and other nonverbal clues to the emotional state of the person who is speaking.

- **Control your self-talk:** Make no call without first reflecting on a prior success. Think and talk to yourself about positive ideas, actions and results. If you don't get the results you planned, waste no time or energy berating yourself. Instead, commend yourself for your efforts, resiliency and persistence, and then immediately begin to strategize for your next success.

**"Most of our so-called reason consists of finding reasons to go on believing as we already do." J.H. Robinson**

## The Top Ten Ways to Get Things Done

Remember, we all have the same 24 hours in a day, 7 days a week, 52 weeks a year. You can't invent new time, so you must manage what time you have. To that end, don't reinvent the wheel. People have been getting things done for centuries and it helps to learn from others. The following are ten of the top ways to get things done that I've utilized throughout my career:

1. **Prioritize:** Continually think, "What is the best use of my time right now?" The new luxury mindset is continually on the go, creating new ideas, always thinking, always doing; they expect nothing less of their sales people.

2. **Practice people power:** Before every major step, think of people you know who may be able and willing to assist your efforts.

3. **Do your homework:** Don't meet with a luxury client without being totally prepared. You should never have to postpone a sales presentation because you did not have adequate information.

4. **Manage yourself:** Stick to your calendar. Respect your to-do list. No matter how many distractions come up, find a way to complete all of your scheduled tasks.

5. **Learn life's lessons:** Make it a habit to write down positive lessons so that subconsciously you recreate them. Study the negative ones to learn what to avoid, and then let them go.

6. **Make the call when it's small:** Don't let a molehill become a mountain. When you take care of problems while they're small, you not only keep them from growing but you also avoid wasting time thinking about them.

7. **Adopt the attitude of gratitude:** Say "thank you" vocally, in writing and through action as often as possible. Few things are as potent as sincere appreciation. Writing your thanks is

good, but a personal visit to say thanks will never be forgotten.

8. **Never publicly show people up, belittle or humiliate them:** They will find a way to get even. In most cases, it will come at a time that's most inconvenient for you. (Avoid it privately, too. It's not good for you, and it's not good for them.)

9. **Take a stand:** We teach people how to treat us all the time, consciously or unconsciously. Why not instruct them from the outset to take a positive, respectful approach to you? It starts with doing the same to them.

10. **Base everything on results:** When you want to lose weight, you use a scale. When you want to save money, you use an account. When you want to see how far you've gone, you look at your odometer. Why should sales goals be any different? Continually evaluate your activities against the standard of whether they are getting you where you want to go. If you're not sure, why keep doing them?

## Other Sales Observations

The criteria clients use to determine how to buy have changed over the years, particularly when it comes to the new luxury mindset. In today's luxury market, it is imperative that we understand how this particular client thinks. Our strategy is simple: to understand clearly what motivates people to buy items that many of us consider luxuries.

The results of a sample group of 33 people,18 buyers gave very specific information.

Here's a quick overview of what Clients buy:

- You

- Clarity

- Comfort

- Experience

- Story telling

- Eye Contact

- What is possible

- A written promise

- The best information

- What matters to them

- Service that over delivers

- Different, Simple and Visual

- The elimination of problems

- Presentations that create images

- Service based on their specific need

- Pointed conversations, brevity and proof

- The reduction of noise around your message

- The power of trends delivered to their product

- First Impressions: Master the first Seven Seconds

- People connected to people they know and trust

- Passion, Strength and Enthusiasm in each exchange

- Influences by bigger names in the industry about you

- Deeper Insight: words, actions and in-depth thinking

- Service or product based on the way they feel about the provider

- Strong impressions with each contact – anything that says "Special"

- Products or services that deliver more service or benefit than the prices

Sometimes in a slow, almost inconspicuous way and sometimes with huge swings, the art of selling changes. Those changes affect how we conduct ourselves from day to day. The most recent revelation is a shift in emphasis. Each era of selling brings a specific focus or emphasis believed to cause success. To better understand sales, it is important that we have a snapshot of our industry over the years. With that understanding we will be able to better position ourselves for the future. The following are the first three phases of the sales process throughout history:

- **Phase One:** Going back to Adam and Eve, the first emphasis was *feeling*. Adam was convinced to go against good judgment based primarily on his feelings for Eve. As we proceed down the history of sales, we come to Caesar. His powerful army camped outside the city and then sent messengers in to spread the word that his army was unstoppable. While Eve used love to sell Adam an apple, Caesar used fear to conquer a city.

- **Phase II:** Then came the Wild West and carnival barkers in loud plaid suits selling health potions guaranteed to cure whatever ails you. They entered towns and sold before anyone who would listen. Their sales pitch was simple: *personal gain*. I find people in many areas of sales who still sell this way. How many times have we all used the idea of the "used car" salesman as a concept we want to avoid?

- **Phase III:** This phase is the Xerox Era. Not because I worked for Xerox, but because they are accepted as a leader in corporate sales training. Other companies offered good training programs. Companies such as IBM and 3M presented great

Emphasize selling *YOUR* vision.

training curriculums. However, Xerox received additional credit because it packaged and sold a product called Professional Selling Skills. During my stay at Xerox there were three versions of Professional Selling Skills. Often companies who did not have training courses purchased or sent their sales teams to training sessions conducted by a division of Xerox. It wasn't just that Xerox sales representatives were successful; their success was also promoted because of those businesses that bought PSS and experienced success.

Somewhere between sales success and word of mouth, Xerox became a leader in sales training. Xerox put me on a path of observation and continuous learning that helped me become a selling professional. Here are just some of the useful nuggets I learned for selling to the new luxury mindset:

- **Set your Vision:** Plan your week before it starts. Sunday is a great day for planning.

- **Clean up:** Neatness saves time.

- **Strategize**: Prioritize your accounts by the value they have to you or your career.

- **Be Curious**: Ask more questions. Listen to the customer's voice, not your own.

- **Get up**: Start each day early.

- **Write**: Develop good penmanship.

- **Entertain**: The most valuable client is the one who will go to dinner with you; anyone will go to lunch.

- **Know your client**: Learn birthdays, anniversaries and hobbies. Know at least 20 things about each client.

- **Solve Problems**: Determine how your business helps people and go help your clients.

- **Study the great ones**: Who do you know in any walk of life that's compelling, that has magnetism, that has incredible people skills? Learn from them. They are selling.

## Time

Take a look at the following chart to compare how successful sales people versus unsuccessful sellers spend their time:

| Non-Successful | Successful |
|---|---|
| • Spend less than 1 hour per day in front of or talking to their clients. | • Spend an average 3.7 hours per day in front of their clients and the afternoon or evening preparing for the following day. |
| • Spend less than 1 hour per month reading or listening to audio clips for self-improvement. | • Spend an average 1.2 hours per week on elements to improve themselves. |

focus

### Selling Summary

Selling is ... an avenue of expression for the talents we are practicing to improve. Set a Vision of where you want to go in life and the talents you need to work on. As we develop these "talents" our focus has to be how we help our affluent clientele.

## The 6th Essential
The Art of Asking Questions

# The 6th Essential

## The Art of Asking Questions

In order to sell information, you must have information. It is of the utmost importance to gather information that allows you to sell according to the client's needs. In particular, selling to the new luxury mindset demands that you be on your toes, do your homework and always, always be prepared.

Selling to the sophisticated client is challenging, at best, and difficult, at worst. The 6th Essential teaches you to focus on what the client knows, because you already know what you know. It is about taking the emphasis off of you and putting it on them.

In short, it is about getting to know your clients better than you know yourself.

### Gathering the Right Information

There is nothing more important than getting client information. In fact, my favorite rant is rather than thinking of *something to say*, think of *something to ask*. A great sales person, Aristotle, in his classic book, *Rhetoric*, stated it in a succinct way: "A speaker who is attempting to move people to thought or action must concern themselves with pathos (i.e., their emotions). If he touches only their minds, he is unlikely to move them to action or to change of mind, the motivations of which lie deep in the realm of the passions."

At the heart of an effective sales call is the belief that nothing is as powerful as an insight into human nature. What compulsions drive a person, what instincts dominate their actions? We must be effective at the art of asking questions. Getting specific information is the most powerful tool we have; it provides us with ammunition that truly motivates people to buy.

I witnessed a display of emotional selling at the opening of a restaurant in Seattle called Planet Hollywood. On the day of the grand opening, streets were packed; traffic had been diverted to side streets and back alleys. There were spotlights, red carpet and the "A-list" included the likes of Bruce Willis, Whoopi Goldberg and Arnold Schwarzenegger.

There were local TV personalities, athletes, politicians and coverage from both local and national news. My first thought was, "Is this a movie premier? Or maybe it was the dedication of a building for higher education?" No, the entire A-list, the spotlights, the red carpet, the stars and the media were there for the opening of… a restaurant.

Unlike most people in the restaurant business, the focus at Planet Hollywood is celebrities. Each new establishment is opened like a movie premiere, complete with movie stars and a red carpet. There are parties, autograph sessions and a feeling that every day inside the restaurant would be exciting. They successfully placed the experience before the food.

Selling in today's market relies on the same principle, but first we must understand the client's needs. With that knowledge, we can then shape our product or service to create a client experience that produces the "WOW" factor. The way we create that experience is by getting more information than our competitors.

We have to become expert at the art of asking questions.

We are looking for what is unspoken: the one, two or three things that cause a prospective client to buy. Sales professionals are positioned so that they must exceed the expectations of every prospect. We must tap into the client's buying emotions, particularly with the luxury market. Just because we would never think of buying a refrigerated briefcase or mink dog carrier doesn't mean that we can't understand why our clients would like to buy them. It all depends on getting the right information.

## "Get your facts first, and then you can distort them as much as you please." Mark Twain

### The Funnel System

If we are going to make a science out of the skill of asking questions, we start with a process described as the funnel system. At Xerox, we learned to ask two kinds of questions – Open and Closed:

- **Open-ended questions allow the client to respond using as many words as they feel comfortable with.**
- **Closed-ended questions limit the customer to yes or no.**

What was never taught was the order and frequency of each question. Enter *the funnel system*. Starting with a series of open questions, you do two things. One, you allow the client to come closer to you. Psychologists have known for years that the more a person talks directly to another individual, the closer they become to that person. Two, as that person becomes closer to you psychologically, they naturally become more open with you.

Coincidentally, the average number of questions on successful calls in today's market is eight per call. Begin with open-ended questions that use the words, who, what, where, why and how.

The funnel system gets its name from analogies that all sales calls should begin with a large space filled with open questions. As the conversation continues, the prospective client grows closer to you, and then the questions become closed or more direct.

Once we have the funnel system down, the next step is to use *leadership questions*. By definition, leadership questions are those that allow the client to see a positive use of your product or service. Leadership questions allow clients to see the possibilities within your product or service. These questions allow the client to sell him or herself. The questions start positive client thinking with key phrases.

For example:

- **What would happen if _____ ?**
- **How would your life (or business) change if _____ ?**
- **When do you most need _____ ?**

Keep in mind that 90% of the sale is information gathering and the sales rep who gets the most information typically wins the sale. Our goal with questions is to know more than the competition.

## The Concept of Dissonance – Our Greatest Sales Tool

In all my years of sales I have seen nothing more compelling than the concept of creating dissonance. When we see something that appears to be an improvement in our life or job, something happens. We become unhappy with our current situation and focus on what could be. This process of disharmony is called dissonance. We all experience it when we do such things as test drive a new car then get back into our old one, try on a new pair of shoes or visit a new home.

Each time we are reluctant to accept our past and reach instead for the future, for what we could have. Nowhere is this truer than with the luxury mindset, who aren't content to get back in their old cars after test driving new ones or even to return to their old homes once they've looked at spectacular open houses.

Clients have the same reaction in the work place. Our goal is to ask questions that allow them to see the possibilities, thereby creating desire for your product or service. Here's why it's even more important in today's market: before the Internet, clients often relied on sales people for information.

Now a client can use the Internet and get as much information as they need. In many cases, they know as much or more about the product or service than the average sales person. In getting the client to decide to buy, nothing is more powerful than creating dissonance by asking the appropriate questions.

When you create discomfort, the client continues to sell him or herself in your absence. Better than PowerPoint and more long lasting than a brochure, the client's need to avoid discomfort is stronger than selling. Your goal is to get customers to make better use of their 60,000 thoughts per day. There is no better way than to get them to think of you as an ingredient to resolve their dissonance.

Learning about your clients gives you a head start.

## Tactics for Improved Listening

How do you see inside someone without staring? The answer: we listen at a higher degree. Much has been written about the power of paying attention and listening. Two of the more powerful strategies are:

1. **Knowing what to listen for:** As the consumer is bombarded with more and more messages (experts say we get 1,500 at rest and up to 35,000 in a grocery store), our focus has to be a laser beam. If we don't create and share compelling messages that are clear to the client, our messages might get lost in a forest of messages. We must learn to watch the buying patterns of our clients. Watching and learning give us a head start. It is clear that we can determine the chances of a sale closing by watching our client's behavior. In a sense, we are completing a puzzle. The psychologist solves a puzzle of life, and we solve the puzzle of how our product or service helps a client.

2. **Echoing:** You must listen in two ways –

    a. **Listen to get an accurate picture of the specific areas where you can help, not sell the client.** If you sell any product or service without first seeking to help the client, you are nothing more than a carnival barker selling snake oil. You have a responsibility to sell with integrity. We must listen in order to sell help, not stuff.

    b. **Listen on a personal level.** Every client has personal accomplishments that are tied to business success. They are not easily divulged. We must listen and learn our client's personal successes that are tied to their business successes. The question is, what have you heard and uncovered that causes the client to feel, see or imagine a different result?

## The Fear of Loss

As we examine listening and questions, I have a question for you: "What causes people to buy more often – the fear of loss or the expectation of gaining more?" The answer is divided.

When a person is buying for personal reasons – a car, clothing, etc. – his or her feelings are based on gain. They are feelings of *what's in it for me*. If a person is buying for his or her company, the feeling is based on avoiding loss.

Here's the second question: "How do most sales people sell?" They overwhelmingly sell on gain! Simply put, our efforts in sales are being crippled because we don't use the most basic of needs. In business, the dominant theme is to protect, to guard, to avoid losing. And most of the sales pitches I have witnessed push "gain." Perhaps we should look at creating a "Loss Test."

In my business of consulting, I typically ask three questions:

1. **When you look back on your investments last year, did you invest more in your business (the building, the equipment, etc.) or your people?**

2. **Where do you think you will get the greatest return, business investment or your people?**

3. **If you did not budget to invest in your people's growth but decided to do so today, where would you invest to get the greatest return?**

This is an example of a loss test. In most cases, the client does not know exactly where they would invest for training. At this point, however, they are ready to listen at a higher level. The major hurdle in selling at this point is having clients that are prepared for your message. It is at that point that you can say and do things to bring them on as clients.

This concept was made clear to me as I read about IBM in the early years. There was an ad campaign that was used to create more sales for IBM's office products division. The ad was a simple black and white layout that read, "No one ever lost their job for going with IBM."

It was clear to me that "Big Blue," IBM, understood how purchasing agents thought. They didn't buy on what they would gain; they bought in ways that would protect their jobs. Today, are you selling on gain or do you understand how to help people avoid loss?

## Selling Summary

**Information is the key to all efficient Luxury Sales. We must get the right information and convert it to emotional motivation for each client. The most important action you can take is to build an emotional connection with the client.**

## The 7th Essential
Customer Attraction

# The 7th Essential

## Customer Attraction

"Everything should be made as simple
as possible, but not simpler."

**Albert Einstein**

Never make another cold call. The ability of customers to get information has lessened their dependence on sales people, particularly when it comes to the new luxury mind set.

This market segment knows what they want, what it's worth and how to get it; your job is to finish the job of convincing them they need it.

Gone are the days of blitzing phone banks or calling strangers. The luxury set relishes familiarity and is eager to do business with people they know. Quality breeds quality; this is no longer about quantity. The 7th Essential allows you to "attract" rather than chase new clients.

## Customer Growth

You are well known in your field, the product you sell is great, and your company's market share has increased for the last two years. Despite these things, however, your future success depends on your ability to find and develop new customers. The one consistent, universal rule of top-flight sales professionals is a well-defined prospecting plan.

Today, effective prospecting is done differently. Conventional wisdom tells us that cold calling, telemarketing and direct mail are effective ways to grow new customers. But the world has changed, and conventional wisdom is often slow to catch up.

The truth is that most business in today's world is done in a less formal manner. Experts agree that conventional methods of prospecting deliver less than a 20% return. On the other hand, prospecting using referrals delivers returns of 79% or higher.

**Phase I:** Spring Board Your Relationships

One of the most common reasons for a lack of success in sales "pros" is that they never fully understand how to penetrate their relationships. Most all sales reps will openly say they have "great" relationships.

My contention, however, is that most of those same sales reps fail to get the most out of the relationships.

Change that today and start penetrating your relationships by following these four simple steps:

1. **Make a list of the clients who rank in your top 10%. Review your working relationship with each; highlight results, problems solved and unbilled extras.**

2. **Focus on the relationships that are successful. Ask each client for one person they know who would benefit from your products and services.**

3. **Explain to each client that their recommendations allow you to spend more time working for them, rather than prospecting.**

4. **Finally, ask each client to phone their contact in order to recommend you and to tell them that you will soon follow-up by telephone.**

**Phase II:** Sell, Serve, Repeat!

There is an unwritten, antiquated "law" that salespeople are somehow more motivated by the thrill of winning new customers than keeping old ones. The best sales professionals, however, know that repeat business is the lifeblood of their careers.

David Butler was a master shoe sales person at Nordstrom in Seattle. He didn't just sell shoes; he was the Tiger Woods of shoe salesmen. For 28 years, he was a Pacesetter (top sales award). For 17 of those years, he was the top women's shoe salesman in the company. During his career, Butler sold more than $20 million in shoes, earning a commission of 10% per pair.

In his biggest year, he sold $865,000 worth of shoes, averaging 50 to 60 sales a day. When asked how he became a shoe millionaire, Butler says, "I try to tell everyone that this did not happen overnight. My success came from repeat business and more repeat business." The best way to generate repeat business is to provide superior customer service.

Current clients are loyal because of superior service, and most will be happy to refer new clients to you. All you have to do is ask. However, you must remember to make good on your promise to spend more time with them. Above all, remember to thank them (with a special gift or a hand-written note) for making those referral phone calls, whether or not their referrals actually turn into new business.

deliver

## Selling Summary

Experts agree that conventional methods of prospecting deliver less than a 20% return. On the other hand, prospecting using previous contacts deliver returns of 79% or higher. Your focus in Luxury has to be "who you know and who they know".

# The 8th Essential
Emotional Advantage

# The 8th Essential

## Emotional Advantage

Of everything written in this book, one item stands above all others: *the value of connecting emotionally with a luxury client*. The new thinking in client mindshare is to avoid the clutter of constant media. That means we must connect with our luxury client in meaningful ways. What became increasingly true after 9/11 is even more so today... few people make a buying decision in front of us.

The approach, then, becomes one of creating ways for the client to think of you and your product *after you leave*. This practice must be very subtle. We should keep one dominant thought in mind: all buyers develop a sense of a product before they understand or consider any facts. Here are a few things you must know about today's buyer and how they view most purchases.

Facts have taken a backseat. More buyers feel before they fact check. They look for a rational reason, then make an emotional decision. "I like it, I prefer it, I feel good about it."

Before seeing something in detail, buyers start to have a sense of what it is. In other words, they feel before they understand. Emotions are more rewarding than logic. It's important to understand the new realities of emotions. We must work out what they mean to our clients, not what they mean to our product.

Perception is extremely important to the new luxury mindset, to the point that a higher price point can actually be a positive versus a negative. A luxury product, for instance, that is priced significantly lower than several of the same models produced by the competition can be "felt" as inferior, despite the product's actual superiority.

Emotion wins out over logic, and the higher priced, similar item is purchased despite the lower cost of the nearly identical item.

In short, the large majority of sales ties directly to "feelings". More and more, the consumer relies on sensory perception, but the best sales companies are training on facts. Buyers have become increasingly more cautious. The mood now is rather than "being sold," buyers want to buy. Today, the number one criterion for a buyer to make a decision is how that item makes him or her feel, regardless, in many cases, of how much it costs.

The goal in effective selling for the luxury market is to put aside our own emotions. It is imperative to be completely in tune with clients and their needs. Once their needs have been uncovered, you must then do the exact opposite of most sales people.

That is, focus on the positive emotion and use that as the basis for selling.

As was found by Martin Seligman in his book *Learned Optimism*, the majority of people have 50,000 thoughts a day. It is probable, then, that at least 90% of those thoughts are negative. To create a long-lasting image that causes a client to buy, we must use their "need" for information to create buying motivations.

## "There is one thing stronger than all the armies of the world: and that is an idea whose time has come."
## Victor Hugo

Unfortunately, salespeople don't have the leverage they enjoyed in the past now that information is readily available on most products. The answer lies in better awareness by building an emotional tie.

Noted neurologist Donald Calne said, "The essential difference between emotion and reason is that emotion leads to action while reason leads to conclusions." In short, people don't buy because it logically makes sense. They buy because, "I like it," or "It makes me feel good" or, simply, "I prefer it."

There are three central concepts that help build that emotion:

1. **Associated Relationships**: This was essentially discussed with the "GIRI" strategy. Simply put, we are all within six contacts of meeting anyone we want to work with.

2. **Sensory Perception**: Emotion is tied into sensory perception. So, we must create a way for people to attach one or all of their five senses to the product. They must become attached to the look, the feel, even the smell of the product. All words and action must lead the client down this path.

3. **Integrated History**: To become quickly attached, most clients must feel some similarity. The quickest way to achieve this is to describe things that tie your past to their own. Great storytelling is a must. Words and images will allow customers to create their own mental nets. When they do, it's assured they will be drawn to the person who created the memory.

In the book *A Million Little Pieces* by James Frey, it opens with a series of events that should have caused suspicion: traveling on a plane, bleeding, with missing teeth and unconscious?

It's hard enough for most people to make a flight and board with everything in order! But most readers, myself included, were just too busy feeling to react logically to the information we were (supposed to be) processing. Because our emotions took us past the facts, many readers bought this story based purely on emotion.

in tune

## Selling Summary

**The goal in effective selling for the luxury market is to put aside our own emotions. It is imperative to be completely in tune with the client and their needs. Luxury clients buy from "want" not "need" and want is developed through feelings.**

# The 9th Essential

## Perspective

# The 9th Essential

## Perspective

Perspective is to take stock and understand where we are in our sales lives. Who are we? What do we represent? What do others see when they look at us? Just as importantly, what do we make them feel?

To reflect on this issue fully, look back and see how we can implement the tools we have learned about; see where they have led you, what you have learned already and what there is still left to learn.

The 9th Essential gives us our personal sales perspective:

### Perspective

After being part of – and coaching – three successful sales teams, I have noticed an average of at least five different kinds of sales focus. Each ties directly to the salesperson's ability to implement new information and grow.

Where do you fall in the following order?

### Phase One:
#### *"What was that?"*

This is the new sales person. Sometimes it's even the sales person who has been selling for awhile, but shows no signs of learning or improvement. The selling world buzzes around them and they ask is, "Who was that? What was that? What just happened?" They never see how to improve; they never learn from their mistakes or their successes.

They live one day at a time. In the majority of cases they wake up each day, go to the office and wait for the day to happen to them. Unfortunately, this group dominates the sales industry and is largely responsible for its bad reputation.

### Phase Two:
#### *"How do I?"*

This group carries a respectable amount of success. With each success they attempt to repeat it and to grow more success-ful. The question is, "How?" They seek to examine and repeat success. They mimic success patterns and skills in other sales professionals.

They show flashes of brilliance. Their sales tend to be errat-ic, up one month and down the next. Typically part of the in crowd within the sales team, they roam the halls with a good attitude and engage in conversations wherever they can.

### Phase Three:
#### *"The next deal?"*

The tide has turned with this group. They have figured out what works. They are professional, focused and systematic. Observation is the cornerstone of their success. When they began their career in Phase I, they quickly learned who and what was successful and made it their own. At Phase Two they made those newfound skills repeatable. It has become their personal system. They own it.

They are visionary. They see opportunity where others don't. Planning is big for them. They plan weekly sales efforts and work the plan. This is the group that does not waste time on the weekends watching television. They actively plan for the next week. Those plans grow from weekly to monthly to annual, and those plans ensure continued success. Because of their focus and their system, this group partners well with upper management as well as clients.

## Phase Four:
### "Knighted?"

These sales professionals view the business of selling as a game. The game is chess, and they look at the next move and how the competition would react. (If I do this, they would do that.) They create change and with that change, old rules don't apply. What's interesting is that this group examines *everything*. The things that work as well as those that don't. They focus on a two- to three-year plan.

They look and act like management but elect to stay in sales, and they understand that income is tied to information. They work intelligently. They are seldom surprised by client comments or actions. In the majority of cases, their experience with clients is one they visualized. They are the highest-paid executives in their fields.

## Phase Five:
### "Is it possible?"

To arrive at level five, you must pull away from the material trappings of sales. Instead, you accept the concept of possibility. Is it possible to use "X" business concept in sales? Is it possible to improve that new likeable sales person?

This level of professional thinks beyond monetary goals. Those have been met. The goals have expanded:

1. **To develop consistent, award-winning accomplishments.**
2. **To help others who show a capacity for sales success.**
3. **Above all, help clients rather than "sell" them.**

They look and act like management but elect to stay in sales and clearly understand that income is tied to information. They tend to work in intelligent ways and are very seldom surprised with client comments or events. In the majority of cases, the experience they have with clients is very similar to the one they visualized. They are the highest paid executives in their respected fields.

## The Plan

The concepts described before this paragraph demonstrate that most sales people don't know where they are in the process of sales development. Where do you fall along that particular spectrum? It is very important to find out where you stand before you can figure out where your clients stand.

Go back, review the previous section and determine where you fall within the phases. With that information, now you can finally focus on where you want to be. At this juncture we have to accept the four levels of "I Know Spice," as described by Jaharie. The concept is that we add spice to our lives in the form of knowledge.

The four levels of spice include:

1. **I Know I Know Spice.** I don't have to think about it. I know that I know, and the function is automatic with me.

2. **I Know I Don't Know.** No emotion exhibited here. I am familiar with this area enough to know that I don't have the specific knowledge.

3. **I Don't Know I Know.** These are the areas where you are surprised. A friend, colleague or business associate makes you aware of some latent talent that you have overlooked.

4. **I Don't Know I Don't Know.** We are completely unaware of what knowledge we don't have.

As you review the four levels, keep in mind that we have to continually seek information and sales excellence if we truly want to excel at reaching the new luxury mindset.

That said, are you planning for your eventual success? The trick

Plan for your eventual success.

is to plan now because everything changes. Most people wait until some great problem presents itself and then fight the problem. Here are the two most important pieces in the planning process:

1. **Sales Business Planner**
2. **Personal Selling Strategy**

Planning your business and career is as important for the veteran sales professional as it is the recently introduced sales rep. The following questions and outline allow you to put serious thought into where you've been, where you want to go and how you want to get there:

- **Career Analysis and Planning**: What do I want out of my career? Specifically, you should think about the fact that a large portion of your life is involved in the way you earn your income. What do you want that career to be like in terms of:

  - **Lifestyle:** Where do you want to live, share, travel and so on?

  - **Work Hours:** What would be your ideal hours?

  - **Income**: How much money do you need over the next five years?

  - **Level of Production:** What do you need to do to accomplish your lifestyle, work hours and income levels?

  - **Clientele:** Who is the ideal client for you, where are they and how can you work with more of them?

  - **Markets:** Where are the current, creative and future areas of business for the attainment of your goals?

    - What has your last year been like?

    - What did you like?

- What would you like to remain the same in terms of the above?

- What would you change in terms of the above?

- What do you have to do to build your career the way you want it to be?

- How will you develop your business?

- **Long-term business development:**

  - Geographic Area? Repetitive approach: Where?

  - Targeted Prospecting? Numbers approach: Who?

  - Sphere?

  - Community / Business involvement?

- **Short-term business development:**

  - Who knows the people I want to do business with?

  - List six companies or people you want to do business with.

  - List two people who can deliver new clients.

  - Define how you can partner with your manager for more sales?

  - Identify accounts or categories you want to go after.

  - Open dialog with your manager about the areas in which you need improvement.

  - Ask if there is business that your manager would like you to follow-up on.

- **Other Factors:**

  - What corporate moves show a need for your product or services?

  - What news stories carry personal information about potential clients?

  - What type of marketing methods will you use?

  - What are your sales follow-up tactics?

  - Where can you write and get an article published?

  - Are there organizations or associations where you can deliver a speech?

  - How can you become more involved in the community?

  - How can you improve your image in the office?

  - What activities do you need to accomplish to develop your career?

  - How much time do you need to schedule for prospecting?

  - How many contacts do you need to make each day.

  - Where do you need education and skill enhancement?

  - In what market will you have the most success?

  - What steps can you take to go from transaction maintenance to relationship building?

- What can you do immediately to improve time management?

- The key Question: Are you willing to do what it takes to develop the career you want?

It is very easy to plan and strategize, but much harder to do the things necessary to accomplish your career objectives. Anything you want out of your career is completely attainable, IF you make the decision to control your business, instead of letting the business control you.

You have the ability to develop your future life and career to match exactly what you want. How will you maintain the discipline and focus that you will need to accomplish your objective?

How will I incorporate:

- **Self talk**

- **Vision**

- **A journal?**

What career skills do I need to accomplish my objective in the shortest time possible?

- **Motivation:** What are the key motivators for my family and me?

- **Prospecting Skills:** What six clients do I want to do business with and who can serve as my GIRI contact?

- **Sales Skills:** What two skills would deliver the biggest return?

- **Presentation Skills:** Have I incorporated the elements of a successful presentation? Do I have the involvement of the prospect? Is there a recent presentation that I can revisit with new skills?

Refine and develop your professional skills.

- **Market Education:** Am I the most knowledgeable in my field? If I were to improve in competitive knowledge, what two areas would give me the most return?

- **Phone Skills:** Does my personality shine and come through on the phone? Am I in business voice or friendly tone?

- **Time Management Skills:** Is my personal vision strong enough to drive me when challenges slow me down?

- **Conversation Skills:** Are my conversations an afterthought or have I confirmed speech patterns that cause me to create real dialogue?

How will I further develop and refine these skills using:

- **Tapes**

- **Books**

- **Seminars**

- **Practice**

- **Web Training**

- What personal education can further develop my skills?

- What is my level of personal magnetism?

- Are my daily goals clear?

- Have I set up the company's compensation plan to help me attain my vision?

- Is this the time I have improved most personally?

## Principles for Better Sales

Remember that selling is a process, not a gift. Particularly for the new luxury mindset, you can't "fake it 'til you make it." You must have already "made it" to approach them, and that means making the time to follow these principles for better sales.

The following are some principles that will help you sell better. The principles alone are not the answer. Use those principles that fit best with your style of selling, and master at least one of the principles rather than become poor at all of them. All of the principles are to be matched with the previous "Essentials" 1-8.

# "No man is an island unto himself." John Donne

### You Are Not Alone

Most of us feel alone in the selling process. The opposite is true. To be truly effective, we have to put together our own team. If you had to get a deal completed in your company quickly, who are the people that would help you? Those are the exact people who must be on your team. Your first sell is to get those people to understand that you have their best interests at heart. Work every day to build that relationship and it will return huge dividends.

The same is true of every sales call you make. You must start at the beginning, with the receptionist, and move to where you want to be from there. Each relationship builds on the other. You can never attain superstar numbers selling alone. You have to develop relationships that sell. Your most effective tools are people who speak highly of you.

After you achieve a great list of contacts and people who believe in you, you will increase your sales by 20%, which soon turns into 30%. Reputation sells you much better than anything else. And sales success will always follow your ability to help people. As you help people, they in turn tell their circle of friends and associates about you. This group acts as your outside team, just as the people in your office act as your inside team.

To create record-breaking sales, you must approach sales as if you are building a team. Treat people with respect and empathy. Treat people as if you plan to have them in your life forever. Don't just build an island unto yourself; build a team.

**"You must adjust . . . This is the legend imprinted in every schoolbook, the invisible message on every blackboard. Our schools have become vast factories for the manufacture of robots." Robert M. Lindner**

### History Has a Declining Value

As I shared earlier, your history does not have to dictate your future. Instead, tap into your potential for growth. Start where you are, not where you've been. Focus on new skills, a new attitude and continuous learning. What's true is that the past does not determine the future; you determine the future. Don't set your future goals based only on your past. Set your goals based on your potential. After all, you can improve your potential.

Spend your time reading, practicing and talking to experts. Take a look at where you are. Give yourself an honest assessment and pinpoint areas of improvement. Find successful people you can observe; not one person to serve as a mentor, several people with varying degrees of talent. Learn tactics that you can use.

### Write and Think

Writing gives you the ability to recognize what you have learned. Planning your future is part of this rule. To have the ability to set a plan in motion increases your ability to achieve it.

The first kind of writing you should consider is personal. Reviewing what we said earlier, use a blank book, journal or diary to track positive aspects of your day. With each day, target three good things that happen to you. Write those items down at the same time each night. As you write, you automatically shed most of the negative thoughts and replace them with positive thoughts. In most cases, these are thoughts you would normally forget. In addition, writing serves as a way to re-enforce positive self-talk.

Next step, let's discuss writing for business. Remember, the one thing I depend on is planning my week before it starts. I plan my entire week. I list each client's name, and then I write how much money I can make if successful. I also write how much money they save or how I can help them. The first writing gives me incentive, the second confidence. The entire list enters my conscious mind. Soon my fears and reservations are replaced with an aggressive, confident sales approach.

The key factor, the most dominant factor to effective selling, is how we think. The personal journal-slash-business journal helps you focus all your mental abilities on the ability to sell effectively. Plan your success: personal and business.

### Finding Number One

Every moment wasted is a moment that you can better spend finding your next best client. The search for your #1 client will bring with it a certain amount of luck. We can ill-afford to waste any time.

To develop a #1 client, start by finding the person who is number one in sales in your office. Talk to them and watch and emulate their sales practices that best fit your style and vision of yourself. It has been my experience that to learn quickly in a new sales environment, glue yourself to the person who has proven that they best understand the process. Find the person who shows through sales results that they understand success.

Soon after you start your sales career, find the top sales person and pull them to a quiet corner, ask them to lunch or, better still, ask to assist them with some of their work. Next ask them for help in becoming more like them.

You will find two things quickly: 1.) Very seldom are people at the top offered or asked for help and 2.) most people who are asked gladly give help because at some point in their career they were afforded the same help. Listen well and pull things from their experience that will help and fit your style of selling. If you have not come up with your style, then use theirs until you do.

Here's what you are looking for: you want to develop as quickly as you can. Many times the best and quickest way to develop is with the help of experience. Once you have the lessons practiced, use your subconscious mind to see yourself in front of customers doing what your mentor taught you.

Start to prospect as soon as you can. Use what you learned to find your first client. You learn how to take care of large accounts with the experience of small accounts. You prepare well, take care of the smaller account, and they, not you, will find you your #1 client.

Look at every account as a life-long relationship. While many will not be, we cannot accurately predict who will be. By taking care of all of your clients, you will be rewarded when you least expect it.

**Know More**

Anyone can stumble on success in the short-term; even lottery winners get lucky sometimes. Long-lasting success comes from knowledge. The knowledge that *got you there* as well as the knowledge that helps you to *stay there*. When people fail it typically boils down to that person not using their full potential. Just think of one person you know who is not living the life they want. If you have them in your mind, apply three words to them and see if they fit:

1.  **Unaware**

2. **Unfocused**

3. **Repetitious**

These three words have one thing in common: there is an absence of knowledge. You will know something that they don't. The fact that you can see their failure is part of your awareness and part of their Unawareness. Due to their unawareness, they are in most cases **Unfocused**. They tend to repeat all the things that make them unaware and unfocused; this makes them **Repetitious**. In most cases you are going to see that skills like prospecting, asking questions, handling objections will never come up. What dominates most failure starts with a general lack of awareness.

How much do we know about ourselves? Do we know enough to properly motivate ourselves daily? How much do we know about our competition?

Make learning a daily thing. Learn, read, and listen to educational CD's, anything that increases your knowledge. If you want to go to heights most of your peers shy away from, learn more and practice that knowledge.

Remember: Success *always* follows knowledge.

### Do The Opposite!

"If you want to get ahead in life, *do the exact opposite* of everybody else and you will probably never make another mistake as long as you live." My grandfather echoed those words often. When I got my first sales job, I finally understood what he'd been talking about all those years.

Most of the sales reps in my branch did what everyone else did. If the majority of the team came in at 8:30 or 9, then the new guys did, too. If each morning was started with lots of conversation around the water cooler, time for actual selling was lost. Here's my point: There are more people who are *not* successful than those who are. If we follow the masses, we will almost certainly fail.

When I conduct assessments, there is always a top 20%. That 20% delivers an average of 80% of the team revenue. The remaining 80% delivers only 20% of the revenue. Again, if we follow the masses, we will almost always be doomed to a life of mediocrity. Your job is to go against common thinking. To reassure yourself, find the few people who are successful and observe and learn from them.

## Celebrate Evenly

When you win you should have worked so hard that you *expected* the win; it should never come as a surprise. Never become overly happy or sad during the process of selling. Work smart, study your craft and when success comes, take it -- but take it in stride. Act as if you deserve that success. And if there is a temporary downturn, take that in stride as well.

Your even temperament combined with continuous learning will take and keep you on the success track. Work smart and learn what professional selling is all about. When you reach that level of competency you will have arrived at the pinnacle, a professional sales executive. And you will be *exactly* what this new luxury mindset is looking for!

## Check the Weather

Weather, at least when it comes to selling, is predictable. If you look for mostly cloudy sales today through the rest of your sales career – you *will* find them. Most of us have heard of self-fulfilling prophecies, and many of us even know how they work. Because we believe something is going to happen, we behave in ways that make it more likely to happen. When it does happen, we say, "Well, sure enough," and our belief is strengthened. Although we may understand the principle, very few of us appreciate the power of our beliefs to affect every aspect of our lives, including the results we get in our business.

In sales as in life, perceptions matter as much as (or more than) facts. What you do with your knowledge is as important as the knowledge itself, and how you make those calls makes all the difference. What's more, all of these things are affected by, often determined by, your beliefs.

For example, given two salespeople with equal experience and knowledge, who will probably be more successful: the one who believes that people are interesting and good-hearted or the one who believes that people are just out for themselves? What about someone who sees change as a threat or someone who sees it as a challenge? Or when things aren't going well, will one who thinks of himself as resilient or one who believes that his career is going down the tubes be more successful?

The answers are pretty obvious. But why are beliefs so powerful? It's because your self-image, the collection of beliefs you hold about the kind of person you are, determines your behavior. In other words, you just naturally behave like the person you believe yourself to be. You don't have to think about it or plan it. It's automatic. It's simply how you are designed. More than anything else, behavior determines results. It's even more important to realize that your beliefs are not written in stone. At some point in your life, these beliefs seemed true or useful, so you adopted them.

Now, I'll bet you're not still wearing the sideburns or beehive hairdo you sported a few decades ago, and you've probably moved since then, too. Yet how many of us still cling to old beliefs that no longer serve us? How many still see ourselves through lenses that were given to us by critical parents, judgmental teachers or others who had no idea what our true potential was?

If you want to move forward in your career, relationships, finances, health, and every area of life, examine your beliefs about yourself. Be completely honest. I have no doubt that you'll discover some beliefs that stop you from growing. You'll probably discover others that are your excuses to fail. And there may be others that keep you from experiencing happiness or taking reasonable risks.

When you find them, challenge them. Think back. Where did you get them? Are they based on fact or fear? Are they about love or limitation? Do they help or hinder you? Get rid of those beliefs that no longer serve you and come up with positive ones to put in their place. Affirm your new beliefs on a daily basis, in thought, word and deed. At first, this may feel a bit strange, but I guarantee you that it will soon become second nature. As it does, you will see your life change for the better, almost without effort.

The following are some beliefs you might want to affirm. As you continue to explore your belief system, try writing down others that address your own personal goals:

- I see all setbacks as temporary and bounce back quickly.

- I enjoy talking with people; the more I listen, the more I enjoy them.

- Cold calling is old school. I use the GIRI system because I am connected.

- The only limits to my success are those I put there myself. I love what I do.

- I am open to new ways of doing things, new ways to think and behave.

- I find something good about every customer, even those I don't sell.

- I am an optimist, and I look forward to whatever each new day brings.

- I use my time wisely, so I accomplish a great deal and still have time to play.

Businesses set annual goals based on the previous year's results. They look at activity as the key to produce increased sales. Two things for you to keep in mind: 1.) Set your goals based on your potential – last year has nothing to do with this year if you tap into your true potential and 2.) Your beliefs will change your behavior, and your behavior will change your performance. If you want unparalleled success, focus first on your belief systems.

# "Courage is not the absence of fear, but simply moving on with dignity despite that fear. " Pat Riley, Miami Heat Coach

### Internal Motivation

Just imagine. What would happen if we could look at every opportunity in life as driving the Rambler down the hill? The reason most people never take their foot off the brake is lack of personal vision.

I have found that sales people never take time to clearly identify the direction of their lives. No time to visualize what they could get accomplished if they planned. Instead, they wake up each day and allow life to happen to them. With no plan, they go wherever life takes them.

Ask yourself some basic questions. What do I want most in life? Who is it that depends on me? If I could have the perfect life, how would it look and feel?

Within these kinds of questions lives your vision. When I find sales people who are not motivated, more than 90% of the time their lack of motivation is tied directly to lack of vision. Vision starts the process of internal motivation. It is the element that causes us to try harder when someone tells us no, to wake up in the morning without the alarm, to work harder and smarter with one recurring thought: Is what I'm doing right now helping me to get to my vision?

We have tons of motivation, but like a cable channel we were too cheap to pay for, it is often blocked. Our ability to tap into vividly described dreams gives us a reason to access our potential. If your vision is a new house, a retirement fund or the care of an elderly loved one, you will work harder. You think and work in ways that allow you to get the most out of you.

Always look at the sales profession as a way to help you reach your vision. Rather than working for the sales goal, work for the house, the family or the peace that comes with helping loved ones. I tell sales people not to work for a check. My advice is to use the job to get things that are important to you.

**Your Master Plan:** Creating a Blueprint for Success

Most sales professionals, whether skilled or unskilled, experienced or novice, dream of superior performance, acceleration bonuses and the corner office. But without a solid plan, the vast majority of these dreams never come true. While they may actually set some goals, most sales people fall short of achieving them because they use the pass/fail system.

Here's how you can reinvent the system of goal setting: Start with the Achilles heel of goal setting, the result. While keeping the end result in mind, focus on the steps you need to take in order to achieve it. If your goal is to lose 10 pounds, the steps might be to exercise for half an hour three times a week, adopt and stick to a low-fat diet and eliminate or cut back on sweets. If your goal is to increase your sales by 50%, the steps could include taking a reputable sales training course, creating a system for letting your current customers know you appreciate their business, and asking current customers for referrals.

When you focus on the process as well as the result, three important things happen:

1. **You gain an increasing level of control over the outcome by gaining control over the process.**

2. **Each time you successfully complete one of the steps, it energizes you to achieve your end-result goal.**

3. **You strengthen your belief that you can achieve goals that may at first seem overwhelming by breaking them down into manageable sub goals or steps.**

It is also important that you know the best way to set specific worthwhile goals. I recommend the following steps:

- **Dream Big:** You will only go after goals that truly *get you excited*. Increasing your sales by 50% is a means to a greater end. When you set a goal, stop and think about why you want it. Once you have the dream in place (larger, more attractive house, college education for your children, freedom to travel, support of a loved one), lay out the steps it will take to get there and start working toward your goals.

- **Write Them Down:** When you write the goal and the steps down, they take on substance and legitimacy. Up to this point, they are still dreams and tend to easily fade from your consciousness. Begin all goal statements with the words "I will…" to reflect your clear intention.

- **Be Specific:** The more specific your goal statements, the more likely it is that you will achieve them. Instead of "I will lose weight," write "I will lose 10 pounds by the first day of spring." Rather than "I will exceed my monthly goal" write "I will generate at least $10,000 more than my June budget," or something equally specific.

- **Review Them Often:** Place your written goal statements someplace where you will see them often: on your desk, the refrigerator, bathroom mirror or dashboard of your car. Review them at least once a day. Monitor and track your progress. Whenever you achieve a significant sub goal or end result, check or cross it off and celebrate.

- **Tell Everyone:** Friends, family and business associates can all help you by following your progress and offering support and encouragement. When times get tough, these are the people who will keep you going.

Goal achievement, then, is a combination of exciting goals, a specific, step-by-step plan of action, written goal statements, systematic tracking and review and a good support system. The difference between failure and success can be traced to poor planning. If you want to achieve a goal and believe in your ability to achieve it, the key to that achievement is *the plan you put into place*.

So, make a firm commitment, take ownership of (accountability for) your dreams, create a specific plan and follow it. Do everything in your power to stay motivated and inspired. If you want to design the life you desire, the secret is good planning.

## Four Secrets of Internal Motivation

The single most requested question during my speaking engagements has to do with motivation. Leaders and managers alike want to understand how to motivate and inspire their people to higher levels of performance. If you will turn back a page or two you will see my comments on vision. Before you can get there, you have to see yourself there.

Earlier I asked you to answer those three basic questions.

1. **What do I want most in life?**

2. **Who is it that depends on me?**

3. **If I could have the perfect life, how would it look and feel?**

These questions are just the beginning of a process to unearth the real reason we work. Let's look at it from a different vantage point:

- **If you have kids, what do you want your kids to have that you never had?**
- **What would you like to share with your parents for everything they sacrificed for you?**
- **What is it you most want to share with your family?**
- **How much would it cost to retire and maintain your current lifestyle?**

The first secret in creating internal motivation is the process of causing in-depth thought. Let's face it, who can motivate you more than you? You talk to yourself more than anyone, you know yourself better than anyone and, more than anyone else, you will most benefit most from sheer exhilaration from accomplishing a dream.

The second secret is really a formula:

**I x V = R**

- **The "I" stands for imagination. Crystallize in your mind the things you want from life.**
- **The "V" stands for vivid. Each and every thought you imagine has to become vividly present in your mind to create the next part of the formula, "R."**
- **The "R" stands for... reality.**

If you want to leave behind your current reality and develop a new reality, then you must follow these steps. You have to *imagine* the reality you want to have. Next you must use your

Use your imagination to your advantage.

imagination for *vivid* recall.

Dissonance is a word that can best be described as disharmony. It is the single most powerful driving force in the area of selling. When we see or imagine something we want, it becomes our vision. Where we live right now is our current reality. Because we have seen something we want in our vision, a feeling of disharmony or dissonance drives us toward it.

Here's how it works if you are selling a client: As you ask questions to understand the client's needs, be sure and ask questions that allow them to envision the future. When the customer sees a better future with your product, dissonance takes over. Long after you have left their office, dissonance will motivate them toward using your product to get to their vision.

### The Question of Why

Suppose for a second there is a highly energetic, optimistic and successful sales person. This person routinely sets new sales records for his company. His life is incredible. All the materials things are in place: a great home, perfect family, the latest cars and beautiful clothing. He lives a dream life.

When you see someone living the life you dream about, let me assure you that success at this level only appears when the "Questions of Why" have been answered. The Questions of Why are the questions that remove the major obstacles, which impede sales growth.

For example: What is the big lesson I can learn to improve my sales? Rather than one big lesson or question, there are levels of sales and they are connected. Your ability to create positive thought is tied to your ability to attract, which is tied to your ability to ask impact questions, which is tied to your ability to develop rapport, etc, etc. To be weak in one area weakens all areas. Practice each discipline of sales and become expert at each.

Why are some people born sales people and others struggling with it? There is no such animal as born sales anything. I have met top sales people in 32 different cities in the U.S. and each of them dedicates many hours to becoming sales professionals. The idea of success without sacrifice is as foreign to the selling profession as it is to the medical profession or the study of law. Now for the good news: The struggle is overcome when you prepare, when you study and when you make your efforts to learn and grow a daily goal.

Why do I feel this on-going nagging doubt? Most people judge their life on their failures. The tendency is to look at life based on history rather than your potential. Doubt is a wasted emotion. Use that same energy to think forward; imagine only the best outcomes. You will be surprised at the accuracy of your goals and vision.

- **Is there success for me?**

- **Is reading and meeting people the key?**

- **Is every person 100% accountable for their success?**

Is there something in the Universe at work against me? This kind of thinking is so different from my previous training, why should I consider it?

Look at the number of times we believed incorrectly. They thought the world was flat, that men would never fly, that women weren't designed for the corporate world, and they believed in Santa Claus. In fact, as we look back in history, it is filled with incorrect assumptions. The real question is whether or not you believe that proper thinking can help you be more successful?

Why should I train when the training appears to work for other people but not work for me? Train not to explore *what doesn't work*; train to find *what works*.

If I adhere to the aforementioned advice will I be able to change? People don't really change. If you follow this advice, you should be able to transform. Not all with one stroke of the mighty pen, but gradually. Each day set a goal to learn one area of focus. As you learn, you transform.

Now, get out there and be the best you can be.

achieve

## Selling Summary

**The difference between failure and success in many cases can be traced to poor goal setting. Because our judgments and actions are mostly self-determined, we can change our plight in life through our own actions. Goal setting for a Luxury Mindset is deciding in advance what you will get used to in the future. It is the one signal that alerts your mind that things are no longer acceptable the way they currently are.**

**The 10th Essential**
Scrap History, Sell Illogically!

# The 10th Essential

## Scrap History, Sell Illogically!

"The key is not the will to win ...
everybody has that. It is the will to
prepare to win that is important."

**Bobby Knight, former Indiana Basketball Coach**

There is a pattern to life and there is also a pattern that sales professionals must follow to achieve success. Unfortunately, it seems that most sales people use patterns based primarily on training or habits developed early in their selling careers while more successful sales representatives forge ahead with new, more targeted strategies.

In a 2005 survey of highly successful sales participants, we found that 83% monitored and changed selling strategies to correspond with changing market conditions. Unknowingly, most less-then-effective sales people use habits that are forged by repetition, supported by incorrect training and more than all of the above ... *practiced by the majority of people in their industry*.

**Become more comfortable in your voice and actions.**

It is our contention that if many highly successful business people gained their success by selectively doing the reverse of what their peers did, then perhaps we should consider the same in sales. Let's start with the simple thought that sales people typically work so hard to sound professional that they forget that most buyers want to buy from those with whom they are comfortable.

Consumers, particularly those in the new luxury mindset, want to buy from people who are "friends". They are so starved for a comfortable relationship that often they buy from people who sound like friends. Sad but true... people overlook all else and replace logic with the concept of comfort.

Let's be illogical and reduce the quality of "business" in our voice. Instead, try to become more comfortable in voice and in actions. Changing this one habit will automatically make luxury clients more comfortable. But there's more: the moment a client hears a voice that sounds more like a friend, they respond with a less business-like attitude, making it easier to influence their decision.

Similarly, we found that the great majority of sales people were forced to use the concept of cold calling because they didn't know any other way to increase business. Study after study has shown that cold calling is only minimally successful.

Most figures confirm that calling on strangers without announcement is only 17% successful. Success here is described as getting a second appointment, not actually making a sale. Let me make a fairly flammable statement at this point --discontinue the use of cold calling. It may seem logical based on prior training, but we suggest doing the opposite.

Doing the opposite starts with understanding that many sales people feel a constant, nagging recurring thought, sometimes called "fear". This recurring thought is the most dominant cause

of failure in the area of selling. Based on our nine years of observations, sales people, young and old alike, support these fears in
five areas:

1. **Lack of understanding themselves, their strengths and
   weaknesses**

2. **Lack of understanding the company they work for – meaning the people in the company**

3. **Lack of understanding the product. Many try to learn all
   company products at once when instead of becoming an
   expert on one product at a time would reduce fear.**

4. **Limited knowledge of the clients and their needs**

5. **Lack of vision of the future. When sales people don't see
   clearly where they are going, the natural tendency is to be
   fearful.**

What we *should* do is scrap history and look for the pattern in
"what's working right now." Equally important, what is "working" in other related and unrelated industries?

The airline industry, for example, scored big with the concept
of frequent flyer miles. Years later the grocery store chains like
Kroger, Ralph's and Safeway used the same concept to equal success, merely changing the name to "frequent shopper." Unless
sales training provides a mechanism that changes as the market
changes, we are doomed to keep pace with failure rather than
outperforming the market. The suggestion here is about identify-
ing our true potential, not our history.

Every year we witness an amazing tradition in our industry.
Companies all over the world sit down and project what the up-
coming year will bring. They start by reviewing what happened
with their sales the year before, then base the new year's projec-
tions on figures like *"10% above last year or 20% above last year's
pace"*.

A better option would be to look instead to their potential, encouraged by tactics like those previously mentioned. If they adopt principles that examine and perpetuate "what works," they'll start a success pattern that allows them to scrap history and grow sales at a pace well ahead of traditional gains of 10 –20% per year.

Thinking logically is what we've all been taught. The new luxury mindset requires a new way of thinking; consider selling illogically!

## vision

### Selling Summary

When most sales people enter the Luxury Selling Market, they don't see clearly where they are going and their natural tendency is to be fearful. The logic from the experiences gained at lower levels of income will not cause success in this higher level of income. History is not the lead factor here ... what may seem illogical is generally the best route.

## The 11th Essential
Brand Logically

# The 11th Essential
## Brand Logically

"The aim of marketing is to know and understand the customer so well the product or service fits him and sells itself."

**Peter Drucker**

Each Sunday the newspaper is filled with countless advertisements to sell products. Just as sales people sell by historical reference, most company advertising is based on past advertising.

Car dealers run ads so similar that many consumers respond by showing up at a dealership that didn't run the ad. But it doesn't stop there. Now there are jewelers, home furnishings stores and even plastic surgeons that run ads with no distinguishing characteristics.

One company that has figured out the concept of branding illogically in the real estate market is Hobbs-Herder Advertising located in Newport Beach, California. Managing partners Don Hobbs and Greg Herder maintain a strong belief in separating their company from the masses of real estate agents and real estate advertising by *branding themselves as the product*.

Don, Greg and their team routinely turn real estate professionals into a specialist in some area of their business. They could be the "Condominium Specialist," "The Waterfront Expert," or "authorities" in any number of vertical markets. Next, Hobbs-Herder builds an effective marketing and advertising campaign for the newly anointed expert.

Included in this approach is:

- **Their Story** – a description of the agent's personal information with a smaller amount of business information. This document is clearly designed to allow the buyer to become more familiar and comfortable with the seller.

- **Collaterals** – each sales piece is based on a consistent theme tied directly to the personal story mentioned above.

- **Ad Campaign** – The agency instructs the sales rep on consistently running an ongoing marketing campaign that may include newspaper and magazine ads, letters, handwritten notes and more.

The result? Sales people who work with Hobbs-Herder set themselves apart from the competition. Consequently, they become the brand, the expert and the leader in sales.

Branding at some level should form a part of all modern day sales strategies. If it's true that we get an average of 1,500 advertising messages a day when we are inactive and well over 3,500 if we are active, then setting up methods to differentiate ourselves is critical. The key question here is, "Can you be a client's sales rep *before* they need your product?" The answer is yes.

This kind of thinking is where the market is headed. Consumers buy the brand NIKE, Mercedes, and Wheaties before they actually make the purchase. It is natural, then, that they buy the salesperson or the image of that salesperson before they actually purchase their product.

Remember that when it comes to the new luxury mindset, perception is reality. I have millionaire friends who've rented Mercedes, leased BMWs and still won't part with their Honda Accords. They know what most people know: a quality car from a trusted manufacturer can get you from Point A to Point Z, trouble-free, for close to a decade.

Those of us in sales view things a tad differently; we recognize the power of perception. We know that Mercedes, BMW and Cadillac sell more than just tires, wiper blades and engine parts; they sell luxury, excellence and trust.

Their brands are built on such luxury-centric keywords as "opulence," "affluence," "sumptuousness," "richness" and even "decadence." To play the part you must brand yourself as the part; don't just *know* your product, believe in your product.

Experience it, value it, recognize its sensibilities and embrace them. Sell as if you live the product; know it inside and out and become the "_____ expert" in your area.

Instead of trying to be a jack of all trades, know one or two of your luxury products and master the art of selling them to the new luxury mindset. Where luxury is considered, quality is always valued over quantity; every time.

strategy

## Selling Summary

**Branding at every level should form part of all Luxury sales strategies. Your success should abundantly produce more success – if you can let the market know about you.**

## The 12th Essential
Beliefs are the Bottom Line

# The 12th Essential

## Beliefs are the Bottom Line

### "Small opportunities are often the beginning of great enterprises."

**Demosthenes**

Most of us have heard of self-fulfilling prophecies, and most of us know how they work. Because we believe something is going to happen, we behave in ways *that make the event more likely to happen*.

When it does happen, we say, "Well, sure enough," and our belief is further strengthened.

But even though we may understand this principle, very few of us appreciate the power of our beliefs to affect virtually every aspect of our lives, including the results we get in our business.

I know there may be salespeople out there who doubt this. They say things like, "Beliefs are baloney. All that really matters are facts." Or, "If you want to be a good salesperson, never mind beliefs. What you need to do is know your product, know your customer and make the calls."

But in luxury sales, as in life, perceptions matter as much as (or more than) facts.

What you do with your knowledge is as important as the knowledge itself, and *how* you make those calls makes all the difference.

What's more, all of these things are affected by, or often *determined* by, one highly mitigating factor: your beliefs.

As you can see I have taken you through the transformation of selling differently to an audience that will make purchasing decisions differently.

This transformation begins with the concept of looking at your current sales opportunity and making what may be considered an "illogical" choice and taking "illogical" actions.

For example, if everyone in your industry rushes to make the first presentation on a RFP, perhaps you should try to be last.

As the last presenter, remember that the client has heard all the numbers, so your strategy should be to get the presentation to come up off the proposal papers and have eye-to-eye discussions.

In each phase of this approach I am suggesting that sales and affluent selling has changed over the last 10 years.

This phenomenon is not just in expensive marketing strategies but a new phenomenon in the area of sales: branding, prospecting, internal motivation and beliefs.

Each of the concepts is tied to selling more effectively and reducing the number of missed opportunities.

Effective selling today and in the near future will be tied to these concepts. If your success in the future is determined by selling, these concepts will be absolutely necessary.

deliver

## Selling Summary

**How we believe triggers how we behave. The formula is that Behavior = Heredity + Environment and from these elements our beliefs are set. To change behavior we must first change what we believe. Following this change, belief will trigger a change in behavior, which in turn, increases our performance.**

**The 13th Essential**
Success Blueprint

# The 13th Essential
## Success Blueprint

"Life is a matter of salesmanship."
**Thomas J. Watson, Founder of IBM**

Every great building begins with a foundation; that is exactly what I've tried to provide in the previous 12 Essentials.

But before pouring the foundation, architects draw up a blueprint so that they can troubleshoot every aspect of the structure and plan every step of the building process.

That is my intention in the 13th Essential: to take the 12 previous steps and move them into an action plan that creates on-going success in the new luxury markets -- and record breaking sales the likes of which you've never before experienced.

on-going

Career planning explores your strengths and weaknesses.

## How To Read The Writing On The Wall Before Its On The Wall

Planning your business and career is as important for the veteran sales professional as it is for the recently introduced sales rep. The following questions and outline will allow you to put serious thought into where you've been, where you want to go, and how you want to get there. Your career is an overwhelmingly large portion of your life, and it deserves well thought out planning.

*My hope is that this guide helps you along this path.*

### Career Analysis and Planning

Sales people don't have jobs; we have careers. For a career to survive, it takes careful planning and an objective journey into your strengths, weaknesses, dreams and desires. So take this opportunity now and explore this section on Career Analysis and Planning:

*What do I want out of my career?*

Specifically, you should think about the fact that a large portion of your life is involved in the way you earn your income. What do you want that career to be like in terms of:

- **Lifestyle:** Where do you want to live, share, travel, etc.?

- **Work Hours:** What would be your ideal hours?

- **Income:** How much money do need per month for the next five years?

- **Level of Production:** To accomplish your lifestyle, work hours and income levels how much do you need to produce?

- **Clientele:** What is the ideal client for you, where are they and how can you think logically about working with more of them?

- **Markets:** Where are the current, creative and future areas of business for the attainment of your goals?

As you explore the above topics, funnel your answers down to pertain strictly to recent events.

- **Short-term business development:**

  - **What can I do today to increase short-term sales?**

  - **What can I learn today to make sales more effective?**

  - **Who can I reach out to today to create more relationships?**

## GIRI Systems:

*Who knows the people I want to do business with?*

The GIRI System of creating relationships versus cold calling is critical to creating a successful career selling to the luxury market.

The following action plan can help you master Go back to the GIRI System and:

- List six companies or people you want to do business with

- List two people by each person or contact who can hand deliver you

- Management – How can I partner with my manager for more sales?

- Identify accounts or categories you want to go after

- Open dialogue with your manager about the areas you need improvement

- Ask openly if there is business that your manager would like you to follow-up on

- What corporate moves show a need for your product or services?

- What news stories bring with them personal information about potential clients?

- What type of marketing methods will I use?

- What are my sales follow-up tactics?

- Where can I write and get an article published?

- Are there organizations or associations to whom I could deliver a speech?

- Where can I become more involved in the community?

- How can I improve my image in the office?

- What activities do I need to accomplish on a DAILY BASIS to develop my career?

- How much time should I schedule for prospecting?

- How many contacts do I need to make each day?

- Where do I need education and skill enhancement?

- In what market will I have the most success?

- What steps can I take to go from Transaction Maintenance to Relationship Building?

- What can I do immediately to improve time management?

**The Most Important Question:** Am I Willing to do What it Takes to Develop the Career I Am Striving For?

This is a very important question that takes serious thought, analysis and decision making, because it is very easy to plan and strategize, but much harder to do the things necessary to accomplish your career objectives.

Anything you want out of your career is completely attainable, IF you make the decision to control your business *instead of letting the business control you*. You have the ability – right now – to develop your future life and career to match exactly what you want.

career

## Selling Summary

**The great majority of selling is done by using "tactics". When you enter the Luxury Market you must embrace "strategies" over tactics.**
**Simply put, you must think at a higher level to be successful – you must understand the overall impact of what you do.**

## The 14th Essential
Perpetual Training

# The 14th Essential
## Perpetual Training

"Do one thing every day that scares you."
**Eleanor Roosevelt**

Selling in the 21st Century depends on our ability to change with what the world is delivering. The key question is, "How do we keep pace with changing sales patterns?"

The secret, as I've discovered, is to *never stop learning*.

The new luxury mindset, in particular, is an exceedingly demanding market to corner; they will not settle for your father's sales patter, let alone your grandfather's.

You can't do things the old way and expect to sell to new markets; you must keep up with the market and, in fact, surpass the market to exceed expectations and predict trends.

One thing about the luxury market is that they enjoy

what's around today, but relish what's just around the corner; give it to them by knowing what's next before they do. That takes **The14th Essential**: *Perpetual Training*.

## Lessons from the Street

When I started my sales career with Xerox, I found that the best way for me to learn was from the sales successes of others. Today, I believe that the majority of my success came from those people. While Xerox gave me an excellent sales platform, people such as Lewis Weiss, Tom Carr, Jim Rout, Ron Fisher, Marcy Wagner and others provided for me to follow and to move forward.

I hope to be an example for you. This book is about you, and ways for you to develop personally and professionally. Remember, success begins and ends with how you feel about yourself.

If it's improvement we seek, we must start with the area that controls self-esteem, confidence and the process of thought. Many of us know that we have the ability to evolve toward excellence. My focus is to help you to know it well enough that the knowledge has an affect on your life and the life of your loved ones.

Just as every great minister receives inspiration and blessings as he writes Sunday's sermon, I know that I will be further inspired as I write to you about your eventual successes.

We both receive gifts. We both see the higher meaning of life and success. We combine our best thinking as we create our best feeling. And in the end, we uncover and explore life's paths to success.

Selling is best accomplished in a comfortable, practiced, almost casual success pattern. My approach to sharing with you follows that same pattern.

Approach the concept of selling with a cool head so that you can see the changes that are coming.

## A Green Light for Learning

Now that you've had a chance to read most of this book, use the following skill builders to increase comprehension and eventually increase success:

- **Highlight in yellow every element that applies to you.**
- **Go back when you have completed the book and highlight in blue each of the yellow areas that stand out.**
- **Now re-read the book, but only the green highlight.**

You will notice that the yellow has been converted to green because of the blue highlight. Each and every green highlight is a "money area" in terms of personal growth. You likely will reap money as well, but my focus here is personal growth.

Read, practice and re-read everything that is green. Now the critical part – when you go back to read what you have highlighted, don't go for "memorizing" what you read. Instead you should focus on "Realizing."

Most of us try to memorize like we were taught in school. We would be better served if we move from *Reading and Memorizing* to *Thinking and Realizing.*

It looks like this:

Reading & Memorizing to ...     Thinking & Realizing

Trying to be better to ...     Becoming better

Reaching a new market means trying, and mastering, new things. Forget your old way of rote memorization that might have worked for passing a quick spelling test on Monday morning but left you unprepared for a pop quiz by Wednesday afternoon.

Now I'm asking you to get away from normal reading and get

into the kind of reading, comprehension and thinking that will make you a great sales person.

## The New Information

Most of what you have read in this book came from people who do what you do: they sell. I focused on what worked for successful people, and in many cases I have repeated the ideas to make sure they have been absorbed.

To learn what works, we study the current effectiveness of the selling industry by conducting interviews with top sales professionals. In our surveys, we found that the majority of sales representatives have a close ratio of less than 20%, and only 50% of those clients represent repeat business in the future.

The sales results companies want most are lost because of the ineffectiveness of their sales team. Fortunately, this condition is correctable.

Many people in sales are just not prepared. They have been bombarded with ineffective tools for selling, ineffective ways to practice new skill sets and ineffective skill sets to practice.

Closing percentages are a direct result of poor sales information being re-circulated in the absence of solid, practical selling information.

The most important area of sales in the 21st Century is proper mental preparation. This has been a story of how the least likely person in the world (me) grew from poverty and ignorance to become a true selling professional.

My hope is that by sharing how I learned and improved in the sales arena, I have somehow helped you become more successful.

### Who's Afraid?

Here's what's real in sales. Fear causes more failure in sales than anything else. The first step in our success strategy is the reduction of fear. If you have had the experience of spending time with a professional sales person, one of the first things you will notice is the absence of fear.

In most cases, their lack of fear is attached directly to their ability. I believe that if you know more about the science of selling, that knowledge will diminish your fear. There are four areas that salespeople need to focus on to eliminate fear:

1. **Knowledge of Self:** When you understand what you stand for, the direction you're going, your goals and your areas of improvement, you become more comfortable.

2. **Knowledge of the company:** As a salesperson you need to know how to get a deal done within your company the fastest way possible. Great salespeople get deals done and they seem to know everyone in the company. They have befriended those people who will help them in a crunch. When you have knowledge like this, it immediately starts to reduce your fear. Not only will you be without fear and be confident in the confines of your company, that confidence will expand to the people that you call.

3. **Knowledge of the customer:** Knowledge is king. The sales person who collects the most information wins. Customers will buy from you because you take the time to understand their concerns. Because you understand their concerns, they see you as a person who is on their side.

4. **Knowledge of the future:** The most motivating factor for a sales rep is to know and understand their mission and their goals and to go after them daily. I am convinced that those sales reps that continually look at where they want to be leave fear behind.

So there you have it, **14 Essentials for Selling to the New Luxury Mindset**. As you go through life, work and your career, I'm sure you will add many more essentials. These, however, make a great foundation for selling in any business, any climate, any time, anywhere – but especially to the new luxury mindset.

From now on, we're not settling for less; we're *Opting for Opulence*.

potential

## Selling Summary

**In the end it's not 1,000 things that cause success, in most cases, it's a few things done well. In the Luxury Market we can learn these ever-changing strategies from disciplined client observation.**

## About the Author: Greg Winston

Greg Winston is a pioneer in the study of high-performance in the area of sales. Since he founded *Sales2sales.com* in 1998, his innovative ideas and methods have had a lasting, positive impact on the careers of hundreds of marketing professionals.

Companies at all levels use his seminars and training programs with proven tools for increased personal and professional success. Local and national sales teams use his Luxury Mindset Research to understand how to better market and sell high end products.

His talents for enhancing motivation and achievement keeps him busy speaking at company, association and volunteer meetings. Greg is one of the few speakers guaranteed to receive a standing ovation with his interactive motivational speech "Creating Unshakable Luck." In his early years Greg began a sales career with the Xerox Corporation and became one of their lead sales professionals.

At one point, his year-to-date sales figures were 10 times more than the average sales representatives. While most sales representatives averaged 105% of budget, Winston set a branch record of 1003%. Immediately following that success he was then promoted to work with new hires. He used those same concepts during stints with CBS Television and Radio then Warner Bros., and now he brings those skills and more to your organization.

In leisure hours his hobbies are reading, working out, computers and shopping too much. Greg makes his home in Laguna Niguel, CA.

To help you get the full value from this book, there are:

**FREE LUXURY SALES SYSTEM RESOURCES**

waiting for you to download at:

# www.LuxurySalesSystems.com

- **FREE Reports and eCourses...an extension of the book**
- **FREE Tele-Seminar with the author**
- **FREE Luxury Sales Tool Kit**

...and other resources to help you apply every luxury sales strategy of this book.

Go there now because every strategy you don't apply is taking money from your future income...plus, you need to hurry, because some resources are only available until the end of the year.

*Go to: www.LuxurySalesSystems.com*

# Continue Your Learning...

Put the *Opting for Opulence* strategies and principles to work in your sales organization. Visit our website and learn more about ways to continue your journey to success.

**Keynote Addresses.** Bring the *Opting for Opulence* strategies and concepts to your next conference. Each presentation is customized to meet your needs.

**Strategic Retreats and Events.** Work directly with Greg Winston to organize and deliver high impact retreats that will create your best sales team ever. You can also qualify to join an exclusive *Opting For Opulence Mastermind Circle.*

**Seminars and Training.** Attend one of our highly interactive programs either at your worksite or at one of our public events.

**One-on-One Coaching.** Customize the *Opting for Opulence* strategies and principles to your specific situation by working with a coach.

*Opting For Opulence e-Classes.* Make the strategies and principles of *Opting For Opulence* come alive in your everyday life. This is an in depth look at what it takes to apply them consistently by using the right thinking process.

Keep growing your luxury sales skills. Take advantage of the tools and resources available to you and your organization. Obtain more information at: *www.luxurysalessystems.com*

## *Opting For Opulence Seminar*

Make the 14 Proven Strategies of *Opting For Opulence* come alive in your everyday life and in your company.

Attend this high-impact seminar and realize these important benefits:

**Accelerate** your luxury sales learning curve exponentially

**Manage** your customers' more effectively to keep the amount they buy and the price they pay moving ever upward

**Expand** your strategic relationships to eliminate all ineffective cold calling

**Identify** the key challenges of your luxury sales system and eliminate them

**Generate** confidence and passion in your sales team

**Increase** your sales team engagement and closing ratios

**Create** accountability in your sales team so they proactively improve the integrity and results of your luxury sales system

This is a one-of-a-kind program and it goes beyond giving you good ideas. It provides you an open road to understanding the new Luxury Mindset. And it gives you the skill set for selling into the luxury market that you can use throughout your career. You can attend a public session or bring this program inside your company. One-on-one coaching is also available.

Obtain more information at: *www.luxurysalessystems.com*

# The Most Incredible
# FREE Book Bonus Offer Ever

**Copy and FAX to: 877-558-0518, Attention: Debbie,**
**- or - take advantage of this offer at *gregwinston.freebookbonusoffer.com*.**

__ **YES!!** I want to take you up on "The Most Incredible Free Book Bonus Offer Ever"

Here's what you'll get:

- **FREE** 60 days of Luxury Sales Mastery Training - At least 1 tele-coaching call every month to unlock the gates and unleash exponential selling success.
- Front Line Expert Interviews - Discover what's working and what's not as we interview top sales leaders and entrepreneurs, getting them to reveal their strategies for creating and maintaining high luxury sales results.
- Mastery Club E-Tips, Articles and Resources - Receive exclusive training material, articles, tips and techniques every single month delivered right to your door along with inside tips on resources and tools to help grow your bank account.
- And an Incredible Welcome Package Valued at more than $149 !!!

To take advantage of **THE MOST INCREDIBLE FREE BOOK BONUS OFFER EVER** you only pay a one-time charge of $8.95 (or $21.95 for Int'l subscribers) to cover postage (but this is for everything. You'll have to experience to believe how incredible this offer really is). Then, after the full **FREE** 60 days of receiving your **ELITE Gold Membership** I will automatically charge you the lowest price that I offer Gold Membership, only $39.95 a month (or $49.95 for Int'l subscribers). And here's the best part, if after the **FREE** 60 days, or anytime thereafter, you want to cancel your Membership, simply give us a call at 877-558-0518, or fax a note to that same number, and my office will **STOP** charging your credit card immediately. No questions, no hassles, no hard feelings. You must be completely satisfied. If not, then I want you to cancel your Membership.

---

Name _____

Business Name _____

Address _____

City _____ State _____ Zip _____

Primary Phone _____ 2nd Phone _____ Fax _____

Primary Email _____

Credit Card # _____

Credit Card Exp. Date _____ CVS # _____

Signature _____ Date _____

# Photo Credits

# BUY A SHARE OF THE FUTURE IN YOUR COMMUNITY

These certificates make great holiday, graduation and birthday gifts that can be personalized with the recipient's name. The cost of one S.H.A.R.E. or one square foot is $54.17. The personalized certificate is suitable for framing and will state the number of shares purchased and the amount of each share, as well as the recipient's name. The home that you participate in "building" will last for many years and will continue to grow in value.

### Here is a sample SHARE certificate:

THIS CERTIFIES THAT

**YOUR NAME HERE**

HAS INVESTED IN A HOME FOR A DESERVING FAMILY

**1985-2005**

TWENTY YEARS OF BUILDING FUTURES IN OUR
COMMUNITY ONE HOME AT A TIME

1200 SQUARE FOOT HOUSE @ $65,000 = $54.17 PER SQUARE FOOT
This certificate represents a tax deductible donation. It has no cash value.

### YES, I WOULD LIKE TO HELP!

*I support the work that Habitat for Humanity does and I want to be part of the excitement! As a donor, I will receive periodic updates on your construction activities but, more importantly, I know my gift will help a family in our community realize the dream of homeownership. **I would like to SHARE in your efforts against substandard housing in my community!** (Please print below)*

PLEASE SEND ME _____ SHARES at $54.17 EACH = $ $_____

*In Honor Of:* _____

*Occasion: (Circle One)*    HOLIDAY    BIRTHDAY    ANNIVERSARY

OTHER: _____

*Address of Recipient:* _____

*Gift From:* _____    *Donor Address:* _____

*Donor Email:* _____

**I AM ENCLOSING A CHECK FOR $ $_____ PAYABLE TO HABITAT FOR HUMANITY <u>OR</u> PLEASE CHARGE MY VISA OR MASTERCARD** *(CIRCLE ONE)*

Card Number _____ Expiration Date: _____

Name as it appears on Credit Card _____ Charge Amount $ _____

Signature _____

Billing Address _____

Telephone # Day _____ Eve _____

**PLEASE NOTE:** Your contribution is tax-deductible to the fullest extent allowed by law.
**Habitat for Humanity • P.O. Box 1443 • Newport News, VA 23601 • 757-596-5553**
**www.HelpHabitatforHumanity.org**

Printed in the United States
141381LV00003B/2/P

9 781600 375095